# THE MARSHALL PLACE CONSPIRACY

the scandal of a property speculation by civic leaders –
its collapse and their ruin – and the architecturally glorious outcome

*by Vivian Linacre*

*celebrating a double bicentenary –*
*the death of Thomas Hay Marshall (15 July 1808) and*
*the building that year of the first houses in Marshall Place*

*vtlinacre@yahoo.co.uk*       *21 Marshall Place, Perth PH2 8AG*

Published by Vivian Linacre

ISBN 978-0-9560082-0-6

Designed and produced by Studio 9 (Scotland) Limited, Edinburgh.
Printed by Bell & Bain, Glasgow.

## Acknowledgments

The immense help given by Perth City Archives and Local Studies in the A K Bell Library is gratefully acknowledged, particularly in arranging and granting permission for reproduction of the eight town maps.

I must also thank the Curator of Perth's Museum and Art Gallery for permission to reproduce five paintings from the City's great collection.

Much encouragement was given by many friends, especially Professor David Walker and Professor Charles McKean. Above all, I thank Margaretha for finding and making our home here.

## A Note on monetary values

*As many references are made to sums of money, we needed a multiplier, in convenient round figures, to indicate roughly equivalent prices today. This is difficult, because (a) an inflationary surge occurred during the Napoleonic Wars – the period in question – and (b) rates of inflation during the last 200 years varied widely among different commodities, ranging from (e.g.) a maximum for land and housing to a minimum for food and clothing. Broadly, a factor of only 4 covers the entire 130 years from 1808 to 1938, but for the 70 years since then a mean factor of about 50 applies. (The third quarter of the last century was the most inflationary in this country's history.) 4 x 50 = 200, which is accurate enough for our purposes. Besides, what an appropriate number for a bicentenary!*

Vivian and Margaretha Linacre acquired 21 Marshall Place in 2004. His 80th birthday coincides with this dual bicentenary. He is President of the British Weights and Measures Association, co-editor of 'Megalithic Measures and Rhythms' (ISBN 10-0-86315-554-5: Floris, 2006) and author of 'The General Rule – A Guide to Customary Weights & Measures' (ISBN 1-978-906069-01-8: Squeeze Press, 2007).

Until now, the scandalous events surrounding the development of the Georgian terraces on Marshall Place, facing the beautiful wooded park known as the South Inch in Perth, have never been revealed. The whole story was suppressed by those in authority, for it was they who were responsible and they who were the ultimate victims.

The episode that coined the term *'bubble'*, to mean a financial crash following an irrational stock-market hyper-inflation, was the notorious *'South Sea Bubble'* of 1720, which was of national consequence, in contrast to the parochial Perth fiasco. Nevertheless, this was definitely a bubble – a speculation by a powerful clique, to exploit a public asset for their personal gain, and which likewise went disastrously wrong.

You may recall that the South Sea Bubble was caused by the South Sea Company's *'folie de grandeur'* in assuming more than half the National Debt (so soon after the 1707 Treaty of Union) in return for large maritime concessions, in addition to the monopoly of South American trade which it already enjoyed. Its £100 shares rapidly rose to £1,000 and an orgy of speculation followed. When the bubble burst, thousands were ruined.

So an alternative title for this book might be **'The South Inch Bubble'!** (*'Inch'* means a small island as the park was once surrounded by water.). For, contrary to all the architectural and civic guide-books, the development of the two classic terraces on Marshall Place – the southern face of the city – was not a well-planned development but a purely speculative scheme by a parcel of rogues on the Council (ex-provosts and bailies) plus a few rich merchants, devised for their private profit.

Furthermore, it was not even their original plan, that had been for seven grand villas, which even the brilliant young architect Robert Reid must have realized was an absurdly ambitious design. What we enjoy today was actually a hastily improvised replacement.

Yet the final plan was a scaled-down version, not only of the housing design, but of Marshall Place itself as merely a component of the magnificent 'Southern New Town' which the young Lord Provost Thomas Hay Marshall and Robert Reid had dreamed of. Even so, Reid's second scheme on behalf of the plotters (an apt word for the traffickers in these plots of land), while superb architecturally, was still hopelessly unsuited to public taste and demand at the time, and even more unsuited to the savage economic conditions prevailing throughout the Napoleonic Wars. Consequently, these twin rows, each of only fourteen houses, took twenty-five years to build, from 1808 to 1833.

The final revelation is that this narrative becomes a morality tale. For ultimately the development ruined all these devious dignitaries, one by one. Ironically, the only member of the élite not embroiled was Marshall himself, who seems to have lost interest once it became evident that only this small scheme was left from his original vision.

Besides, he was already too heavily committed to the 'Northern New Town', based on his patrimony. There he and Robert Reid created an elegant suburb around Rose Terrace, regrettably named after his wife (or her mother?) Rose Anderson. His divorce proceedings distracted and almost demented him for seven years, which included the whole of his first term as Provost (1800-02). So this is a domestic tragedy as well as a story of municipal corruption and a fortuitous triumph of urban planning.

Corner of Rose Terrace, Perth.

Marshall Place as it is today (2008).

# Contents

# Illustrations

All photography by the author © 2008.

Portrait of Thomas Hay Marshall by David Junor (c.1806)

# Chapter I

## THOMAS HAY MARSHALL
### – *a tragic hero*

Minutes of Meetings of the Council of the Royal Burgh of Perth provide a detailed and seemingly exhaustive account of the Council's transactions, ranging from Petitions to the Sovereign and large-scale new developments to petty details of municipal house-keeping. The four chief pre-occupations throughout were: chronic concern with a perennial burden of debt, maintenance of civil order, upkeep of the Town's churches, and, above all, its own annual elections and dealings with the Magistrates.

Until the Reform Act of 1832 revolutionized local government – conferring the vote on all householders paying rates of £10 or more – Perth Town Council was wholly hierarchical. The Council numbered 26, comprising 14 merchants and 12 tradesmen. These were distinct castes, the tradesmen comprising 7 Deacons and 4 Councillors nominated by the trades guilds plus the Trades Bailie, the other Bailies being merchants. There was not even a Committee structure until the 1820s.

So the Council was responsible for – and was required to approve – all official business, whether the erection of a lamp-post, appointment of a church minister or schoolmaster, or grant of a small pension to an injured employee, as well as major issues such as administration of justice, public health and morality. Whenever an extraordinary or long-term project arose, the Council nominated an ad-hoc Committee, with effectively delegated powers, usually comprising the 'inner house' of former Provosts, present and past Bailies and Deacons, possessing extreme latitude and authority.

A coterie of families virtually monopolized civic government – an oligarchy known as 'The Beautiful Order'. In 1825 Tom Moore famously translated the City of Edinburgh's motto '*Nisi Dominus Frustra*' as 'Unless you are a Lord you cannot get on here' – likewise in Perth unless you belonged to that magic circle. As George Penny's '*Traditions of Perth*' (1836) narrates:

"This abominable system, calculated for the complete subversion of the liberties of the citizens, existed in all its splendour in the eighteenth century. There was a particular *junta* that kept the civic honours among themselves. The Provost was nominally elected every year; but to hold office for only one year was felt a disgrace. He was, therefore, re-elected for the second year, then the former Provost returned for another two years.

The Dean of Guild was elected in much the same manner, from a leet *[list]* sent down to the Council. The Trades Bailie was also chosen by the Council, from a leet chosen by the Trade whose turn it was to have the Bailie. The Treasurer was chosen alternately from the Guild and Trades side of the Council. The Magistrates were elected on the first Monday in October, and the Deacons of the Trades were elected on the Wednesday following. The Trades which sent Deacons to the Council were the Hammermen, Glovers, Shoemakers, Fleshers, Wrights, and Tailors. The Weavers, though a corporate body, had no seat at the Council board – they having at some point either neglected or been defrauded of that privilege. The Brewers and Dyers were incorporated with the Guildry."

In 1787, fifteen years after the opening of John Smeaton's new Tay Bridge which transformed the Burgh's economy, a member of this élite, Thomas Anderson declared in a memorandum to the Council that he had:

*"lately purchased from Mrs Miller her half of the Blackfriars lands which, with his own half [which he had acquired from John Richardson of Tullybelton], he would wish to offer to the public for building on, and upon such a plan as might be perfectly agreeable to the Town, for which purpose he would wish to bring all the grounds within the Regality."*

Now Thomas's father, John Anderson, who had been a business partner of a notable Provost, William Stewart, married Catherine Sandeman (1717-97), a daughter of the Bailie Sandeman who had been taken hostage by the Young Pretender's army in 1745. John Anderson's sister Mary likewise married William Sandeman of Luncarty (1722-1790) and Thomas's sister Catherine married one David Lindsay whose son Henry married Jane Sandeman, granddaughter of William Sandeman, of course!

So young Thomas, with his brothers and brothers-in-law, inherited a large fortune, in the linen trade as well as in property. A partner in the Town's Mills with ex-Provosts Fechney and Ramsay, he could also afford to dream of a 'New Town' on his Blackfriars lands, the site of the former Dominican Friary. He discovered and recommended to Perth Council a 23-years old Edinburgh architect, Robert Reid (1774–1856), who formed an auspicious partnership with Thomas Anderson's future son-in-law, Thomas Hay Marshall – only 4 years older but died 48 years earlier – which turned that dream into reality, creating Rose Terrace (named after Thomas Anderson's wife or daughter), as well as Atholl Street, Place and Crescent, facing North Inch, later extending to Barossa, Stormont and Melville Streets.

David Graham-Campbell's booklet: *"Thomas Hay Marshall and the making of Georgian Perth"(Edinburgh, 1985)* provides much valuable information, but a biography of Robert Reid is still awaited. How Anderson met Reid and why he was so impressed as to entrust all this work to such a young architect from another city remains a mystery, as does the bond between Reid and young Marshall.

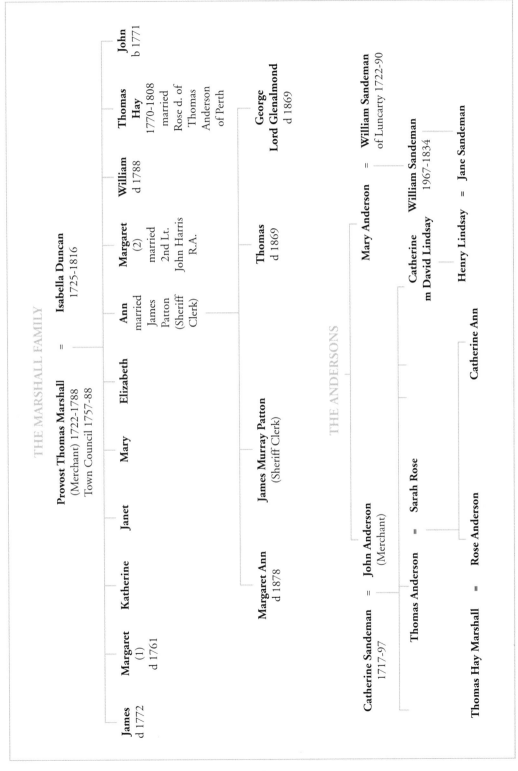

THE MARSHALL FAMILY

**Provost Thomas Marshall** = **Isabella Duncan**
(Merchant) 1722-1788      1725-1816
Town Council 1757-88

James
d 1772

Margaret
(1)
d 1761

Katherine

Janet

Mary

Elizabeth

Ann
married
James
Patton
(Sheriff
Clerk)

Margaret
(2)
married
2nd Lt.
John Harris
R.A.

William
d 1788

Thomas
Hay
1770-1808
married
Rose d. of
Thomas
Anderson
of Perth

John
b 1771

James Murray Patton
(Sheriff Clerk)

Margaret Ann
d 1878

Thomas
d 1869

George
Lord Glenalmond
d 1869

THE ANDERSONS

**Catherine Sandeman** = **John Anderson**
1717-97                    (Merchant)

**Thomas Anderson** = **Sarah Rose**

Mary Anderson = **William Sandeman**
of Luncarry 1722-90

Catherine
m David Lindsay

William Sandeman
1967-1834

**Thomas Hay Marshall** = **Rose Anderson**

Catherine Ann

Henry Lindsay = Jane Sandeman

— 3 —

Thomas was 'born into the purple' of Perth, the eldest surviving son of Thomas Marshall, who had been Provost in 1784-86 and who was instrumental in the founding of the Academy, the paving of the High Street and the planning of the first houses in Charlotte Street, that short thoroughfare which afforded the vital link between the Bridge and the North Inch. With Thomas Anderson, Marshall Senior was a founding director of the Perth Banking Company in 1787 and its first president. His eldest son James died in 1772, the second son William took over the family's linen business and partnership in the pioneering new cotton mill at Stanley (with William Sandeman and the great pioneer of automatic spinning machinery Sir Richard Arkwright) but died in the same year as his father, 1788, leaving Thomas Hay Marshall in sole charge at the age of 18.

Why both brothers died in their youth, and Thomas survived only to the age of 38, is undiscovered. According to the City Archives' register, his death in 1808 was caused by "water in the chest" – probably the outcome of a long, possibly congenital, illness. (Death certificates were not required before 1855, the only records being kept for the parish by the local kirk. All such surviving material was deposited at Register House in Edinburgh, but unluckily nothing is available from this period for Perth.)

Losing two brothers and his father, and finding himself alone with the family textile business to run, must account significantly for the fierce energy and single-mindedness with which he attacked life for the next twenty years. When he was born, the tenth of her eleven children, their mother Isabella Duncan was 45 years old, an exceptional age for child-bearing at that time, yet she lived to the great age of 91, but sadly outliving most of her offspring.

Within two years, young Marshall had succeeded as a member of the Town Council and followed as a director then as president of the Perth Banking Company. In 1791, at the age of 21, he became the Town's Treasurer and the following year a Merchant Bailie. That was the year of his inevitable union with Rose Anderson; as dynastic a marriage as any between provincial commoners could ever be; and, like so many ordained unions, it proved domestically disastrous.

## The Mismatch

But Marshall seemed scarcely to notice, for as always his mind was concentrating wholly on money and municipal power. By 1796 he had assumed responsibility for the Blackfriars development, retaining for himself a magnificent house on the near corner of Rose Terrace, and working closely with his friend Robert Reid throughout. The feus were laid out as had been prescribed by Thomas Anderson. Rose Terrace was designed as thirteen lots, each purchaser being obliged to build, within two years, a house of stone with ashlar front and roof of blue slate, containing a vault and a ground floor with two upper storeys and garrets above.

Each householder had 112 feet of land behind his house which was not to be used for any noisome or noxious trade such as soap or candle-making or for boiling yarn, slaughtering or coppersmithing….and each was to lay paving stones in front of his house and form a grass bank sloping down to the still open Balhousie lade (mill stream) that ran between the Terrace and the North Inch.

By 1800, at the age of 30, Marshall was Lord Provost. The direct financial rewards of office were negligible, the Lord Provost's annual salary being just £8.06.08 (1/3rd of £25), so his main income necessarily derived from real estate. In 1801, during his first term as Provost, the Duke of Atholl appointed him a Depute Lieutenant of the County. This holograph letter from him in the City Archives (PE15 Bundle 1), dated 1 May 1799 and addressed to "The Honourable The Town Council & Magistrates", shows how wealthy and powerful he had become:

"I propose making an opening for a new street of fifty-six feet in width through the grounds of Blackfriars and parallel with Methven Street, to communicate with the Town of Perth a little to the West of the Tan Work. I hope you will allow me to throw a bridge across the Town Lade *[the course of the future Mill Street]* for that purpose, which shall be done at my own expense and under the direction of any person you may be pleased to appoint." **This was the origin of what became Kinnoull Street, named diplomatically after his friend the Earl of Kinnoull; later extended southwards by the formation of Scott Street to link with Marshall Place.**

The Registers of Seisins show that on 30 October 1802 he acquired 9 acres "of the lands of Blackfriars on the North side of the Turnpike Road leading from Perth towards Dunkeld and Crieff", plus 5 acres on the South side of the said road. Land was still the index and only reliable store of wealth in that precarious age.

The solidarity of the clique who ran the city, even a generation earlier, is well illustrated by the list of subscriptions for building the new Tay Bridge (1766-71). For among the scores of individual contributions ranging from the Earl of Kinnoull's donation of £500 to £1 (multiply by say 200 for today's money) are a group who each gave precisely 20 guineas (£21), including Thomas Anderson, William Sandeman, George Fechney, Thomas Marshall and James Ramsay, most of whose names recur throughout the saga of Marshall Place.

## *Unrest at Home and Abroad*

War against France and Spain emptied local garrisons of the regular soldiers that had served as a police force, so companies of local militia had to be raised – particularly in Perth, where riots fomented by radicals were a constant fear.

The perceived danger was not only sporadic violence erupting out of economic unrest – the seething despair of destitution – but even a national revolution imitating and abetted by the French. So in 1794 Provost Ramsay undertook to provide three companies of 38 men each, two commanded by Marshall and his brother-in-law James Paton (Patton) respectively and the other by one Captain Charles Archer, of whom much more later. The approved uniform featured red jackets with blue facings and white breeks. Men who joined were exempt from conscription into the hated militia and possible posting overseas. So volunteers were readily available in 1797 when, because of the worsening Continental situation, a second battalion was raised, comprising four companies of fifty men each, plus a regimental band.

Provost Fechney (or Faichney) had originally been in command, but not for long. As George Penny narrated: "When mounted on his steed, dressed cap-a-pee, his large head rammed into a small helmet, from whence his cheeks hung down below his chin, a short tight jacket, which disdained to make any apology for his haunches, and an immense paunch descending to mid-thigh, all announced the Colonel more conversant with civic rites than the toils of war….on the first inspection, feeling inadequate to the fatigue of putting the corps through their evolutions, the duty was devolved upon Major Marshall. This drew some observations from the inspecting officer, which led to the worthy Provost's immediate resignation of the command, to which Mr Marshall succeeded."

As early as 1 September 1797, Major Marshall wrote to the Duke of Atholl as Lord Lieutenant to enquire whether men of his Regiment "called upon to drill and mount guard in the absence of regular troops are entitled to pay for their time?" There must have been a very quick response, for five days later he wrote to the Scottish military chief Col. Rooke, reporting on arms and accoutrements sent by order of the Duke to Perth. 100 stands of arms had been despatched to Dunblane, 100 stands to Coupar Angus, 40 to the Nairn Volunteers and 200 retained by his own Perth Battalion.

During a brief interlude of peace in 1801 they were stood down but reconstituted under Marshall's command on resumption of hostilities in 1803. Marshall's monthly return dated 18 January 1804 for the 2nd Regiment of the Royal Perthshire Volunteer Infantry (City Archives ref: PE66 Bundle 33) shows a total complement of 395 comprising:

364 Rank and File, 19 Sergeants and 12 Officers, who also included two gentlemen named David Walker and William Stewart (son of the former Provost?), both of whom, along with Ramsay and Archer, had recently acquired or were about to acquire house plots in Marshall Place, as we shall see shortly. Neither military training nor aptitude was an essential qualification for a commission in the militia but, as will soon become evident, participation in the Marshall Place project certainly helped.

Marshall's brother-in-law, James Paton, who had married his sister Ann, and a powerful lawyer who became Sheriff Clerk and Clerk to the Lieutenancy of the County, rose to Lt.Col. in command of the 1st Battalion of the RPVI, leaving Marshall in charge of the 2nd Battalion. Paton made a point of writing to the Duke to ensure that he had no objection.

They were finally disbanded in 1806 after government withdrew all pay and allowances, because fear of invasion had receded following the victory at Trafalgar. Officers had never drawn any pay for themselves, putting it into a contingency fund, which it was decided to donate towards the building of Marshall's new Academy. According to Graham-Campbell, this had amounted to the vast sum of over £1,000, but the figure of £400 mentioned later ('The Seminaries') is much more reliable.

## Declaration of War!

Marshall and his bride lived, during their few years together (1792-96), in the first-floor flat of one of the new houses, no. 4 Charlotte Street, owned by one George Gray, whose brother Andrew had the shop below and whose great-niece was Effie Gray – the future wife of firstly John Ruskin and secondly John Everett Millais – of whom more anon.

But Marshall's marriage soon ended in the divorce court, following his petition on account of Rose's adultery. Cited first was The Rt. Hon. Thomas Bruce, 11th Earl of Kincardine and 7th Earl of Elgin (1766-1841), immortalized by the notorious 'Elgin marbles', who for the period in question was lodging on the opposite side of Charlotte Street, while commanding his own regiment of Fencibles.

Cited second was a Dr William Harrison, Lieutenant Surgeon to the Durham Rangers and Princess of Wales' Light Dragoons.. Marshall brought the action in 1796, whereupon Rose decamped to Edinburgh and thence to London, running up more debts in his name. Yet nearly six exhausting years later, on 12 January 1802, she was still complaining in court proceedings of his "withholding payment of £100 aliment due in August last", to which he bitterly responded on 19 January, only seven days later, readily offering to pay but only if relieved of liability for her debts: *"without the hazard of being subjected in a second payment to the Respondent's creditors"*.

Meanwhile, before the great Lord Cullen (Lord in Ordinary) with Lords Meadowbank and Methven, she had complained of **his** separation from **her**, and that throughout the three years until August 1799 he "did not advance a single shilling towards her maintenance". She had first applied for £150 p.a. *(say £30,000 today)* "which sum corresponded to the interest *(@ 5%)* for her dowry" of £3,000 *(£600,000)*, but the requested aliment was modified by the Commissaries to £100p.a. Evidently, he did pay from 1799 to 1802 but had not for the earlier years because – quite apart from the need for an indemnity – the promised dowry had actually never been paid. Yet she still pursued him, through her lawyers, claiming that:

*"...he is a very considerable merchant in Perth and the first magistrate of the town. He is besides proprietor of some very valuable property called the Blackfriars in the immediate neighbourhood of Perth, on which a new town is daily building, and the property of several houses, one of which belongs to himself...estimated at £5,000. And he has also drawn a dividend from the estate of the petitioner's father to the amount of upwards of £1,000...yet he was not even paying the £100 a year due to her."*

To which he replied: *"his income is not such as to enable him to pay even the £100... The fact is that his income consisted almost entirely in the manufacture of linen and cotton cloths which as for the last two or three years has been attended with loss. He has further suffered considerably by a concern in a cotton mill at Stanley. He has been rather unsuccessful also in the speculation of building houses adjacent to the North Inch; and his situation is on the whole such that his present free income is scarce £200 per annum."*

Here's his own admission, as Lord Provost, of a personal financial involvement in "the speculation of building houses adjacent to the North Inch". But that was enough for him. As we shall see, the speculation of building houses adjacent to the South Inch he left to his cronies.

It is no coincidence that, immediately after his wife's desertion, from 1796 onwards, Marshall threw himself into his local military career, alongside his municipal affairs. The physical and social activity as well as the exercise of authority, must have afforded him immense relief.   Letters were still being addressed to him in Charlotte Street in 1798, two years after the separation. The marriage, of course, had been childless.

Just before his wife absconded, he had suffered another crushing blow; the discovery that her father's estate, which had always been regarded as flourishing, was bankrupt.   Marshall was ranked as creditor even for her tocher (dowry) of £3,000.   Rose's misconduct had become flagrant:   she was actually discovered in bed with another officer of the Durham Militia, John Cooper, who was lodging in her father's own house, and she took lodgings herself to be near Lieutenant Edgar of the Royal Artillery at "the fort or battery between Newhaven and Leith".   With this evidence, Marshall renewed proceedings and at last secured his divorce in December 1803.

## Peace at a price

So ended eleven years of marriage – over six of them spent in costly proceedings.   This was only one year after completing his first double term as Provost.   Yet less than five years later, at the age of only 38, he was dead.

The crucial issue in the earlier divorce proceedings had been whether the two cited paramours (bearing in mind that adultery then was a criminal offence) should be summoned as witnesses or not.   He wanted them to take the oath; she was desperate to keep them out of it.   On 15 February 1798 a fresh judgment was delivered:   "The Lord Ordinary having again considered the case answers replies and whole proceedings with the memorials for the parties and having advised with the Lords, refuses the Bill and remits to the Commissaries with this instruction, that they sustain the objection to the admissibility of the Earl of Elgin and Dr Harrison."

This disgraceful decision spared them (and her) the ignominy of cross-examination, and likely charges of perjury – which could still and perhaps should have been brought retrospectively once her notorious behaviour had finally elicited the decree.   Why should Marshall have had to suffer another five years of worry, expense and deprivation of any private life, for no purpose except to protect the guilty parties?   But for this ordeal, would he have died so young, and how much more might he otherwise have achieved?

He died at Bowerswell Lodge on Bowerswell Road (the old highway to Dundee, which went round the back of Kinnoull Hill), where he could be comfortable;  rather than move into the Rose Terrace mansion, in which he had lost interest ever since discovering that his wife had used it in his absence for secret assignations.

## Too busy for Living

Indeed, he might have already sold it, since apparently it was not mentioned in his will.   But he was perhaps intending to move into Thistlecroft (so says Penny), another house which he had newly completed, straight down South Street, with a magnificent formal garden looking across the river, which his brother-in-law James Paton (Sheriff Clerk) inherited and renamed variously Marshall Lodge or Marshall Cottage. It was eventually demolished to make way for the new Queen's Bridge and replaced by the Norie Miller Gardens.

Nor could he enjoy part of the estate at Glenalmond that he had over-stretched his finances to acquire from the Duke of Atholl. Among his correspondence in the National Archives is his last letter to the Duke, dated 6 April 1808, explaining that – until he had to travel to Edinburgh to consult the doctors there – he had been confined to his room ever since they had last met, and therefore was unable to do anything about the sale of the Glenalmond property as desired to meet the demand for £5,000 which was soon due; so would His Grace kindly write to request the Directors of the Perth Bank to renew the Draft for another 6 months? On the 29$^{th}$ of that month, having returned to Perth, he wrote to Mr Pallister at Dunkeld House, the Duke's Agent: "I had a letter from His Grace last night agreeing to an offer I made of £12,000 *(for Glenalmond)*….I must stir myself to procure the needful from some of my friends – I think Mr Paton may be able to assist me. I feel much better than when I had the pleasure of seeing you, and you may suppose that it will add much to my pleasure to see you again now that I can have the satisfaction to converse with you without pain. The Duke's friendly letter has done me more good than all the Doctor's stuff put together."

But he had to write again to Pallister, some six weeks later, on 15 June 1808, advising that he had been once more confined to his room, yet still hoping "to get out again soon", and meanwhile begging him to retrieve the letter that he had sent to the Duke when he made his first purchase in Glenalmond, in which he had bound himself to get above a certain figure for the whole estate, "as this transaction is now at an end." So was his life, for that was exactly a month before he died.

Yet he had attended a Town Council meeting on 6 June, and on the 24$^{th}$ sent a note to Robert Peddie, the Town Clerk: "A sight of you would do me good. I really wish you would come over and give me the news." He simply would not let go. As late as 1 July he wrote yet again to Peddie: "Old Farquhar has drawn upon me for two years' rent of Huntingtower for which he says I am liable. Now, as you have the charter, I beg you will send it by the bearer that I may be certain – as I think – that he is wrong. I wish to see the book where the Blackfriars feus are, which I will return in a day or two, as I understand Hepburn wishes to deviate from the elevation of the end house in the Terrace." *(i.e. at North end, originally intended to match that at the South end which formed part of his own house)*

Did he discover whether or not "he was wrong"? We cannot tell, for a fortnight later he was dead.

A pathetic footnote is provided by a Memo. dated 23 June 1810, written to the Duke from Marshall Cottage by T. M. Harris, son of Lt.Col. Harris and Marshall's sister Margaret, seeking support for his admission to the Royal Academy at Woolwich.

Having changed hands at least once following Marshall's death, Bowerswell became the tenanted home of John James Ruskin, father of the great art critic and historian, and his family, until acquired from their second or third landlord by George Gray in 1827 (in which year the new Kinnoull Church and the Murray Royal Hospital were opened). By a strange coincidence, the new owner was a nephew of the George Gray who had been Thomas and Rose's landlord in Charlotte Street.

Euphemia Chalmers Gray was born on 7 May the following year, the eldest of fifteen children. Two young brothers, George and Everett, who was 26 years younger, were the boys in Millais' painting '*The Boyhood of Raleigh*'.

(Effie's mother was a daughter of Andrew Jameson, Sheriff Substitute of Fife; his son became Andrew became Sheriff Principal of Aberdeenshire; his son Andrew became Sheriff of Perth and later Lord Ardwall; and his son John became Sheriff Substitute of Midlothian & Haddington. What did they all find to talk about: did any of them ever have an original thought? Effie's more adventurous spirit must have derived from her father's side!)

Effie and young brother George stayed with the Ruskins in London *en route* to and from school. So it was unsurprising that on 10 April 1848 Effie married John Ruskin, eight years her senior, in the new Bowerswell House that her father had spent three years building. (That same year, Ruskin published his great work, '*The Seven Lamps of Architecture*'.) His parents did not attend the wedding, because they thought the Grays socially inferior and also because Ruskin's grandfather (John Thomas Ruskin) had cut his throat in the old house in 1817 in the very room where Effie was born eleven years later, so John's mother refused to set foot in the new house. Effie left Ruskin in London in 1854 for Bowerswell and was granted an annulment only three months later.

So on 3 July 1855 Effie enjoyed a second wedding at Bowerswell. (Her infant brother Everett was baptized immediately following the marriage ceremony.) She and Millais produced eight children, yet Effie was always ostracized in London because of the Ruskin stigma. But they frequently holidayed at Annet Lodge, just behind Bowerswell. Millais died in 1896, and Effie on 23 December the following year, at Bowerswell. No fewer than fourteen of the Gray and Millais families are buried in Kinnoull Churchyard.

The house remained in the Gray family's possession until after the death of Effie's brother Melville Gray at the age of 98 as recently as 1946 – that was 118 years after the birth of his sister! Her brother George had meanwhile also died at Bowerswell aged 95. But it was almost destroyed by fire in 1892 and rebuilt again. It is now a retirement home and also Perth's World War II memorial.

In 1870, Gray had commissioned Millais, his son-in-law, while President of the Royal Academy, to produce the famous fourteen drawings of New Testament parables reproduced in stained glass on the huge West window of the nearby Kinnoull Parish Church – designed by the Edinburgh architect William Burn and opened in 1827. This is the very picturesque building, in a wooded setting on the East bank of the river, looking across to the Tay Street esplanade.  It has recently been extensively restored, urgent work having become necessary for the window's conservation.

But while the Victorian Bowerswell House is so celebrated for its connections with the Ruskins and Millais, the former Bowerswell Lodge as the home of the dying Thomas Hay Marshall is almost forgotten.  For he had practically no private life during the last of the three phases into which his adult life of only twenty years so neatly divides.

First, supporting his father's failing linen business and growing real estate interests, entering into public office and an arranged marriage; second, a welcome interlude with the militia as a distraction from the prolonged agony of divorce proceedings, while pursuing high civic office and replanning the city; and third, once he was free, concentrating largely (very confidentially) on dealing in land – both as agent and on his own account.  For the market was so depressed that bargains were plentiful.  But the Duke and Marshall were not pursuing a calculated twenty-year investment strategy – there was simply no other safe refuge for their money.

His principal client was the Duke himself.  The National Archive lists 25 letters from Marshall to His Grace, all concerning real estate negotiations, within the twelve months from 12 September 1804 to 16 September 1805.

On that first date he felt free to enquire whether the Duke thought the Earl of Mansfield might be interested in purchasing the Glenalmond Estate.  But at that time David Murray, 8th Viscount Stormont and 3rd Earl of Mansfield, was busy rebuilding Scone Palace, to a design by William Atkinson (1773-1839), "who displayed in this, his first major commission, his own rather stolid interpretation of the picturesque Gothic manner of his master James Wyatt" *(John Gifford).*

By the way, considering that: (i) Atkinson was just one year older than Reid, (ii) Scone's period of construction (from 1803 to our *annus mirabilis* of 1808, with additional work extending to 1812), coincided with the early stages of Marshall Place, and in such close proximity,  (iii) each was working on his first major commission, and (iv) like Reid, Atkinson later undertook many other grand projects for exalted clients in the region – such as the remodeling of Taymouth Castle for the Earl of Breadalbane (1818-22 & 26-28) and Rossie Priory for Lord Kinnaird (1807-15) – for all those reasons they must have been well acquainted.

Indeed, Marshall too had extensive dealings with the Earl of Breadalbane, writing to him as early as 13 October 1794, soliciting his intervention with the Duke of Richmond "to procure for my brother-in-law Lieut. John Harris of the Royal Artillery, at present stationed at East Bourne in Sussex, either Adjutant or Quarter Master to the Fifth Battalion which is immediately to be formed, under the command of Major General Drummond which, if he is so fortunate as to get, will render him comfortable in his situation for life – he has the honour of being personally known to the Duke and has already applied to His Grace by letter; but unless backed by high interest, is afraid he will not succeed – on this account I have been so bold as to apply your Lordship, as I well know your Lordship's recommendation would be sufficient.  May I therefore hope your

"Perth from Barnhill",
by Macneil Macleay (c.1846)

Lordship will take the trouble to interest yourself in this business, as there is no time to lose and it will be gratefully remembered both by my friend Harris and your Lordship's servant…..." (Already mentioned was the petition to the Duke of Atholl, sixteen years later, by Harris's son!)

That was addressed to the Earl's London house in Wigmore Street, London, and the date of receipt on the back of the carefully preserved envelope shows that it took only four days to deliver – about as quick from Perth by horse as by today's second-class mail.  Other correspondence from Marshall to the Earl was addressed to houses on Park Lane or St James's Square in London or to his Scottish home at Taymouth Castle.  On 18 April 1804 he wrote:

"Presuming upon your Lordship's former kindness, I beg leave to solicit the honour of your business in Perth which, if your Lordship is pleased to honour me with I shall execute with fidelity and dispatch – the young man your Lordship formerly employed in this place having become bankrupt.  I have the honour to be, my Lord, your Lordship's faithful and much obliged servant……….."

And on 26 June 1807:  "Having been very lately informed that your Lordship had had it in contemplation to make a purchase of that part of Glenalmond which remains unsold, which lies so contiguous to your Lordship's other lands, I take the liberty of mentioning that if you still continue to have the same views, I shall very readily, and without any delay, afford your Lordship every information regarding the property that may be necessary, or in my power, as well as communicate the offers I have already received for it, which may serve to give your Lordship an idea of the value put upon it by intending purchasers;  and should your Lordship, after due deliberation, make an offer of such a price as, upon the most mature calculation I shall deem to be adequate, I will exercise the full powers I possess of immediately closing a bargain. I have the honour to be….." *(Like the others to London, this was also received in four days)*

We might condemn such importunate letters today as touting or, at best, canvassing, but were then considered perfectly proper, provided the niceties of social rank were strictly observed.

But a touching note on 4 November 1804 (to Taymouth):  "If your Lordship will order the Drummers down to Perth, I will get them properly instructed and shall look after them particularly during the time they are quartered in this place. *(They were, of course, boys.)* I do not know of any person qualified to teach both drum and fife, but I will make particular enquiry, in case your Lordship does not approve of sending them here.  I have the honour to be….."

I cannot resist adding another letter to the Earl, dated 2 April 1804, that was necessary but somewhat impertinent, so Marshall got a friend (Colin Campbell) to write:  "I find the men have a great aversion to be armed with pikes, and as most if not all of them are already tolerable expert marksmen, it would be a pity not to supply them with fire arms, especially as pikes may be distributed to great advantage amongst other bodies of men entirely unacquainted with the use of a musquet.  Will your Lordship therefore have the goodness, by writing to Lord Moira or by any other mode of application which may appear preferable, to get this great obstacle to discipline removed?  The tailors are busily employed in fitting the clothing, which I hope will be very soon finished – but what signifys our having red coats upon our backs – far better to have good arms in our hands."

This same letter showed the rivalry between the fencibles and the volunteers, saying that he "would prefer to face the enemy with the disbanded and degraded fencibles than with volunteers of any description whatsoever".

On 28 September 1805, Marshall took instructions from the Duke of Atholl in the sale of the corn and paper mills at Ruthven. Industry was depressed. An entry in the 'Seisins' records that on 29 September 1806 he dealt with James Paton in:

"the superiority of parts of the Barony of Huntingtower viz. Newhouse, 3 Parks and parts of Blackruthven – part of the Estate of Strathardle called Finnegeand, Polgorum, Bellno and Knocklea with the Glenings pasturages and grazings thereof, parish Kirkmichael; with the lands of Lethindies and Kinchraggan, Downies Easter and Wester, and Dalick or Salick, with the Mills & salmon fishings, parish Crieff." He succeeded in acquiring the policies of Huntingtower from the Duke. Finally, as late as 21 May 1808, less than two months before his death on 15 July, he obtained the redemption of two loans of £1,000 and £500 secured on the "ground of the South division of Rose Terrace…with the houses thereon…"

But this impressive property portfolio, including also his late father's tenements on the north side of the High Street and the portions of Blackfriars that he had bought from Thomas Anderson and from Anderson's trustee in bankruptcy, were offset by the massive sums still owed to the Duke and to a host of other creditors, far in excess of the amount due from his debtors (see below).

How tragic that this brilliant, revered, civic leader should have died so young and so lonely, childless and with constant financial worries! His first term as Provost (1800-02) overshadowed throughout by painful and expensive divorce proceedings and his second term (1804-06) beset by military demands and dire economic conditions, that he achieved so much in such a short time was nigh super-human. He seemed determined to burn himself out – to throw himself furiously into Council business in order to escape from his private tribulations.

**It is tempting to draw comparisons with his contemporary William Pitt the Younger (1759-1806), who also died young, childless, lonely, heavily in debt – and likewise after a second term of office for the identical years of 1804 to 1806.**

Marshall dated his Will 7 April 1808, barely three months before his death. The witnesses were Provost Laurence Robertson (acting as a magistrate) and brother-in-law James Paton, Sheriff Clerk of Perthshire, who was also executor and (apart from a few minor bequests) sole beneficiary – which is rather odd. But there was nobody else in Marshall's life. Paton and Robertson certified his death on 15 July and executed registration of the Will, together with the Inventory Valuation and Deed of Settlement on 8 October.

So Paton acquired the Lands and Barony of Huntingtower, the parts of estates acquired from the Duke of Atholl at Strathardle and Glenalmond, also: "all and whole those parcels and portions of the Blackfriars of Perth still belonging to me…purchased and acquired by me from

Thomas Anderson and William Marshall, Agent for the Bank of Scotland *(who, as we shall see, originally bought Lot Five on Marshall Place but sold it on to Bailie John McEwan)* at Perth, Trustee of the Sequestrated Estate of the said Thomas Anderson *(also Thistlecroft and properties on the North side of High Street by the Mill Lade)* …and all and sundry other lands and heritages and all debts of money heritable and moveable crop stocking furniture books silver plate bank notes money and in general all my goods means and estate of whatever denomination which presently belongs or shall belong to me at the time of my death, together with all bonds bills dispositions and generally every other title deed for conveying the lands, debts sums of money and others hereby disponed and particularly…the effects and sums of money which shall be contained in any Inventory to be signed by me…"

It's fair to say that he didn't leave much out!

Marshall bequeathed four annuities: one to his mother, aged 83, for £150, £200 to his 37 years-old brother John Marshall (a comfortable income, suggesting that he was incapacitated and therefore totally dependant – two other brothers having died young), and £15 each to his servants John Reid (aged 54) and Elizabeth Wilson (45).

The first section of the Inventory (prepared by one "James Christie, Licenced Appriser") relates to "Goods belonging to the Cotton and Linen Manufacturing Concern" – what was left from his father's business – amounting in value to £1,957.01s.09d. Such a large sum would have suggested that it was thriving, except that over 90% of it (£1,789) consisted of "Grey Cloth in the Warehouse". Since this is treated as part of Marshall's personal estate, he must have long been sole proprietor, for what it was worth.

Then the second section relates to "Utensils and room furniture" amounting to only £19.16s.00d, but the third section devoted to "Wines and other articles in the cellar" is much more interesting. The sheer quantities are astonishing.

"116 Dozen Good Port Wine" (1,392 bottles) at 36/- (£1.80) per dozen; and "2 Pipes Port Wine"= 1 tun = 4 hogsheads = 8 barrels = 256 gallons = 2,048 pints! And what about "21 Gross & 5 Dozen empty bottles" – i.e. 3,084 bottles – valued at £35.06s.09d, which (you will be pleased to learn) works out at exactly two-pence three-farthings per bottle. But over what period could one man and his guests consume such a vast volume, and why keep thousands of empties that were worth more than a servant's annual wages? Total value of this section was £576.13s.07d – ie. £110,000 or more today.

The fourth section concerns bedroom furniture, bedding, linen, etc. Again, the quantities are stupifying: 4 Dozen Towels, 10 large Table Cloths & 10 smaller, 42 pillow slips; in addition to 2 feather beds, a hair mattress & a straw one. Total valuation £147.09s.04d.

Next came silver, china and cutlery, much of it very fine, the outstanding item being a Silver Tureen valued at £120. Total valuation £191.05s.09d.

The sixth section, "A parcel of books" merits only a single entry with a valuation of £8. Marshall was too busy to read for pleasure or for learning. Next was "Wearing apparel, Watch, Pistols, etc., with a total value of £37.12s.00d.

So, including a few odd items, the total valuation of his "Moveable Effects", as certified by James Paton, amounted to £2,938.01s.02d.

There then follows a meticulous account of "Debts owing to the Deceased as at the time of his death per List thereof – £2,822.00s.02d." Evidently, he had ample notice of his impending demise, ensuring that his affairs were in perfect order. Added to that amount are numerous other possessions – company shares, silver and furniture in other premises, goods belonging to the Cotton & Linen Manufacturing concern, etc. – excluded from the Inventory of personal effects – bringing the credit total to £9,391.17s.02d.

Next, an equally copious list of "Debts owing by the Deceased", amounting to £22,750.09s.01d. Adding other liabilities (including capital valuations of his four annuities – the calculations of which revealed how short were life expectancies – and provision for taxes) raises total deductions to £26,240.06s.07d, exposing a "Deficiency" of £16,848.09s.05d.

What was the purpose of the Will and Accounts, if James Paton was inheriting everything? It was much more than a book-keeping exercise – a stock-taking of his legacy – for apart from needing to detail all the debits and credits, and address that huge 'Deficiency', a 'deponement' (deposition) was required to fix the amount of duty payable, based on that total of £9,391.17s.02d, i.e. for within a statutory band between £7,500 and £10,000. But in this case, "There is not free Executry of Personal Estate, the same not being sufficient to Discharge the claims upon it and which by Law are chargeable thereon, All which is Truth as the disponent shall answer to God", So the Deed of Settlement was evidently granted without delay.

Marshall was owed a sum of £225 by His Grace the Duke of Athol, yet he owed the Duke £12,150, as to £6,000 payable Martinmas 1808, plus £6,150 payable Whitsunday 1809. He owed the Heirs of Peter Duff ("Merchant in Perth") £3,200, the Revd. John Dow £2,010, Robert Peddie, the Town Clerk, £826.00.06d "including interest to 15 July 1808", "Messrs Innes Beveridge & Co. of London – To Bill for Mr Marshall's accommodation £1,500" (but that's about £300,000 in today's money: but when did Marshall ever have to incur such a debt in London? Or was this a *financial* "accommodation", i.e. a loan, for continuing to repay his ex-wife's bills, and did Paton have to settle it?

Marshall even owed to James Paton himself the colossal sum of £1,813.08s.11d "for attested accounts 2 April 1808", which Marshall would surely have queried were he still alive – or was this figure inflated in order to keep the Estate Valuation under the £10,000? While allowing for the undoubted affection and trust between the two men, it is clear that Marshall had little choice in naming his beneficiary!

However, all this is exclusive of Marshall's property portfolio, about which, at the time of his death, we know little beyond the mentions in his wholesale bequest to Paton. Is there no Estate Valuation Roll nor even a Register? What did he actually own – how much had he actually paid for? What was the gross value and what the nett value after deduction of unpaid balances of prices? He had apparently decided to pass the lot over to Paton, skipping the whole issue of valuation, and leave him to sort out the outstanding Bills.

By the way, it is mildly curious – though entirely irrelevant – to note that 1770 was also the birth-date of Wordsworth and of Beethoven, both of whom were at the height of their powers in 1807-08, when 21-28 Marshall Place was building and Thomas Hay Marshall was dying. (It is equally irrelevant and interesting that in 1808 the Slavery Act came into force – the world's first abolitionist legislation.)

Marshall's death must have been long anticipated, for 'The Scots Magazine' had already prepared an obituary that appeared in its issue for the same month of July 1808, which concluded:

*"it is impossible to turn the eye to any quarter in this town or its environs without some remarkable remembrance of Provost Marshall coming into view. He had a particular pleasure in planning out, and a particular energy and vigour in executing, whatever appeared to him as calculated to ornament, improve or be in any respect beneficial to his native city. Schemes which, from obstacles of various kinds, would have appeared impracticable to most men, his prudence, exertion and perseverance speedily effected."*

# Chapter II

## MARSHALL PLACE
### – the plans unfold

Periodic town plans are indispensable sources of hard evidence relating to progress of development at exact dates. Rutherford's map of **1774** illustrates Perth as still a mediaeval city with only a few dwellings over-spilling to the north and west; but it does show Smeaton's new Bridge and George Street providing the necessary approach.

Then in **1787** the plan from Buist's survey showed – in crude, diagrammatic form – a 'New Street' roughly along the line of the future Marshall Place and others indicating the routes of the future William and Scott Streets.

The projected route along the line of what became Marshall Place defined itself readily enough, from the dock on the West bank and skirting the Northern boundary of "Cromwell's Citadel". Significantly, this map shows the entire section from Scott Street in the west, extending beyond the Edinburgh road to the river in the east and from the as-yet unformed Marshall Place one block north to the as-yet unformed William Street, roughly divided into blocks to feu for potential development.

Only five years later, MacFarlane's plan dated 4 June **1792** depicts no new building except on Charlotte Street by the bridge, but reveals the breaching of the town walls to improve traffic flows, the widening of the ports and removal of the Cross; and shows, feintly super-imposed, the lines of the future Marshall Place and King Street as well as the new turnpike road to Dunkeld – to replace that running across the North Inch - and the New Town of Blackfriars laid out diagrammatically to form what became Barossa Place, Barrack Street, Atholl Street and Rose Terrace.

The principal subscribers to the elaborate Dedication on this plan, headed by Provost Alexander Fechney, include the 22 years-old Treasurer Thomas Hay Marshall, with Bailie James Ramsay and Convener John McEwan, both of whom were future purchasers of Marshall Place building lots. John McEwan became Trades Bailie in 1795, 1799 and again in 1803.

A folded plan, engraved in **1805** by Wm. Kirkwood, faces the title page of a book by James Cant entitled 'Memorabilia of Perth' which was published locally in 1806 by Wm. Morison.

The dedication reads:

*"This Plan of Perth with the Intended Additions & Improvements is Respectfully Inscribed to Thomas Hay Marshall Esqr."*

Clearly, this tribute commemorated his finally demitting office as Provost in that year. The purpose, in depicting several buildings and other features – some of which materialized years later while others never did – was evidently to exhibit Marshall's continuing aspirations. So Robert Reid's great pride 'The Seminaries' is illustrated here with a decorative sketch, while Marshall Place is shown as a single block extending from Scott Street to Princes Street (no Nelson Street for another year), on which are roughly depicted seven building plots – five detached villas plus one at each corner – other than which there is no indication of any building in the whole area south of Canal Street. For Kirkwood's sole concern was to highlight the commitment to develop along Marshall's new road.

**As confirmed in Cant's text: "A row of villas has been planned at the north end of the Inch, and the lots disposed of; but none are yet built."**

So Reid's original plans, to provide for the erection of seven mansions on Marshall Place, had been scrapped by 1806. This is corroborated by George Penny's 'Traditions of Perth', which narrates that: "About the year 1802, an excambion was made with the proprietors of the gardens on the north side of the South Inch and, on the west, with the Glover Incorporation, by which the marches were lined off straight, and the ground of Marshall Place feued out. **This line was at first sold in seven lots for villas, but never was built. The feus were given up, and the present plan adopted."**

How strange that none of the civic or architectural guides explain that what was built resulted from 'Plan B' and that 'Plan A' is never mentioned! Even posterity has helped the speculators to cover the story up.

The next and most important plan, in **1809** (one year after Marshall's death), is from a survey of the Town by Robert Reid himself. Only four years Marshall's junior, Reid was destined to live far longer and become as important a figure nationally as Marshall was locally. His plan reveals a great deal of what Marshall had accomplished, much of it with Reid, within those seventeen years since 1792: a doubling in size of the North Inch, the building of Atholl Street and Crescent, Rose Terrace with its fine central block to house both Academy and Grammar School, Mill Street and St John Street in the town centre and, on the south side, Canal Street and King Street as well as Marshall Place and surrounding thoroughfares.

## The Dream of a "Southern New Town"

Gone was Buist's notion of development east of Princes Street down to the shore; though the coal and wood yards survive. But gone too were the mediaeval Spey Gardens – ripe for development! For Reid had conceived an even more ambitious scheme, what was called a southern 'New Town' – to match the northern 'New Town' on Blackfriars. Bounded by Marshal *[sic]* Place, Princes Street, and the future Scott and Victoria Streets; this whole rectangle was shown quartered by the sudden insertion of Nelson Street (North-South) and the future William Street (East-West), so as to form four outward-facing squares. (William Street, of course, was not named until after William IV's accession in 1830, a few years *before* completion of the Marshall Place development, nor was Victoria Street named until the Queen's accession in 1837, a few years *after* its completion.)

But one prominent feature of the 1809 Plan was the afore-mentioned Charles Archer's magnificent new villa and formal gardens fronting Victoria Street, on the axis of Nelson Street, intended to command this glorious southern vista. An entry in the Town Chamberlain's Accounts dated 11 August 1806 reads: "from Chas. Archer purchase money for 2 Lots in Canal Street £75." This double feu ran through from the south side of Canal Street to the north side of what became Victoria Street. On that noble site today stands a 'Matalan' retail store – quite the most hideous building in Perth.

Reid's master-plan was stupendous, comparable to his simultaneous design (with William Sibbald) for the Northern New Town in Edinburgh. It is astounding that such a utopian vision was conceived and projected despite the delays to his plans over the previous six years and the severe economic conditions of the Napoleonic Wars. Moreover, it stirs the emotions to reflect that Reid's survey and plan must have been commissioned and discussed months earlier, before Marshall's death – the two having been such close collaborators.

Certainly, this southern 'New Town' extended far beyond what the Council had approved only seven years earlier, which was only for building seven large villas along a proposed new road. But their master-plan was doomed. Reid must have known as much, even as the drawing was sent to the engraver, for it shows only one small block of eight terraced houses newly completed, at the western end of Marshall Place to the corner of Scott Street.

How strange, again, that there was never any official record of this scheme for two great garden squares! Reid must have designed it purely as a tribute to his dying mentor. Historic appreciation of its merits as an exercise in superb urban planning, nevertheless, is long overdue.

Construction was initially progressing from west to east, in line with the Lot numbers, contrary to the street numbers given to the houses later, so that the eastern terrace eventually comprised nos. 1-14 and the western terrace 15-28; those first eight houses becoming nos. 21-28.

**Therefore, since these eight houses had not appeared on the plan of 1806 but were shown accurately on the plan of 1809 produced by the actual architect, their date of construction is definitely fixed at 1808, i.e. immediately following completion of the Marshall Place roadway** (*Council Minutes of 28 March 1806*) **and the change in design envisaged by James Cant in 1805.** (*Minutes of 6 January 1806*)

But this radically revised scheme could not have been adopted until the Council had devised and improved a plan to form Nelson Street, with all its financial implications, yet no record can be found of any Council Minute or other form of resolution to create this North-South divisor or of the necessary expenditure. The conclusion clearly is that the Nelson Street scheme was an integral part of the scheme by the promoters for replanning the Marshall Place development.

So how were the original Lots, which had been feued for the proposed construction of seven large villas, along a continuous frontage of precisely eleven chains (11 x 22 = 242 yards), secretly transformed into two terraces, each of fourteen houses, and divided by the insertion of Nelson Street?

What were the conveyancing mechanics for the surrender of those seven feu-charters, and how were the feu-duties re-allocated, while providing not only for the sacrifice of a strip of land to form this new North-South thoroughfare, but also for the capital cost of the work? Who paid for the construction of Nelson Street and was the required strip of land wholly extracted from the central Lot Fourth – and, if so, how much of it was left? How much of Lot Third was apportioned, with Lots First and Second, to this first block?

But the heart of the mystery is why it all needed to be done so quietly, quickly, unanimously and amicably – and how that was accomplished – considering the strong personalities and their individual financial anxieties and the impossibility of arriving at a perfectly equitable partitioning and redistribution of obligations.

One of the proprietors must have been exceptionally powerful and persuasive, not only to hammer out such a complex deal and get the others all to agree without any complaint or delay, but also to suppress publicity or disclosure of the financial details.

**Above all, why was it imperative that this whole complex legal and financial restructuring should leave no record?**

Was it Marshall himself who master-minded the whole project while – as we shall see – refraining, unlike his closest colleagues, from taking any personal financial interest in it? Was he the independent assessor, broker, sole arbiter and censor? No! He would not undertake such a heavy, onerous burden, to add to all his other commitments, at such a late stage in his working life. So suspicion must lie elsewhere – among the protagonists.

At all events, Reid's Town Plan of 1809 was clearly designed as a testimonial to Marshall's achievements and to promote this grand design of four garden squares, even though it was no more than fantasy. Mercifully, Marshall took that dream, unspoilt, to his grave in the adjacent Grey Friars burial ground.

By 1809, moreover, the 'Town's Lade' had been mostly culverted. This was originally a defensive ditch which evolved into a canal that ran roughly three sides of a square, entering near what is now the town end of Smeaton's bridge, westwards along the line of Mill Street, south along Methven Street then east along Canal Street to rejoin the Tay by the 16th century harbour, just north of Greyfriars – which, as the name implies, was formerly the site of a Franciscan Friary. The lade served as the tail race of the City Mills which in the 18th and early 19th centuries were vital to Perth's economy. Indeed, the Rev James Scott wrote in 1796 that Perth's main manufacture was "linen, and of late, cotton cloth." And it had been the foundation of the Marshall family's fortune and misfortune.

But by 1809 Europe was at war again. In that same year Napoleon defeated the Austrians at Wagram and "British expeditions were twice forced to retreat from the Continent; Sir John

Moore gloriously from Corunna, the Duke of York ingloriously from the Dutch island of Walcheren. The newest General, Arthur Wellesley, and his Spanish allies beat the French at Talavera." *(Robert Hurd: 'Robert Peel', 2007)*

Meanwhile at home, in that same year of 1809, seditious gossip surrounded Mrs Clarke, the Duke of York's mistress, who was accused of selling Army commissions, and the country was in turmoil. Within three years following Pitt's death in 1806, Lord Greville had come and gone as Prime Minister and so had his successor the Duke of Portland, leaving the equally useless Spencer Perceval in office, until in 1812 he was shot dead in the Lobby of the House of Commons by a businessman who had been ruined by the continual wars – and who was cheered in the streets on his way to Newgate prison. In 1810 the mob rioted for four days in support of the radical MP, Sir Francis Burdett, erecting barricades in Piccadilly. The succession of Lord Liverpool as P.M. in 1812 was hoped to restore some stability, but that year the economy slumped because of the war's accumulated damage to European and American markets. Government was constantly fearful of a civil uprising. There cannot have been a less propitious time for any expensive housing development.

And yet, by the way, despite domestic turmoil and foreign war, that first decade of the 19th century witnessed in Britain the most glorious flowering of practical genius in any country in all history. An engraving in the National Portrait Gallery (by George Sobel & William Walker) depicts an imaginary gathering at the Royal Institution of 'Men of Science Living in 1807-08' – that is the very title – the first years of building in Marshall Place and the last years of Marshall's life. This galaxy included:

**John Dalton, Humphry Davy, Wiliam Congreve, Richard Trevithick, James Watt, Thomas Telford, John Rennie, Alexander Nasmyth, William Jessop, Sir Marc Isambard Brunel, John Playfair and Nevil Maskelyne. They were the pioneers of the Industrial Revolution – indeed, of the modern world – and of those twelve, no fewer than five were Scots.**

## Hard Times

1814 was the year of the great flood from the overflowing of the Tay (the worst in recorded history – to a depth of 23ft OD) which drowned the city and the Inches. Then, after 1815, demobilization of the army and navy – together with an ever-growing flood of immigrants from the Highlands and Ireland – caused massive unemployment. 1815 also witnessed riots in the streets of Perth – attributed to "the discontented state of the working classes, particularly the weavers" – which greatly alarmed the military as well as civil authorities. For the local textile industry – so vital to the fortunes of a large section of the merchant class – had collapsed.

It was cotton that had brought the industrial revolution to Scotland – more than thirty years ahead of iron – but the new spinning mills were largely dependant on export trade which was cut off from 1803 onwards.

Consequently, the northern half of Reid's scheme, between the future William and Victoria Streets, was soon abandoned. Even worse, the town plan by the great cartographer John Wood dated **1823** – fourteen years later – still shows only those eight houses on the western terrace. However, six new houses had been built at the opposite end (modern nos. 1-6) from the corner of Princes Street. So how did that section relate to the original Lot numbers? Did this block at the Eastern end comprise the whole of Lot Seven or also part of Lot Sixth? Still only fourteen houses had been built and fourteen more yet remained to be built, in order just to complete the two terraces on the main frontage.

**All the evidence so far indicates 1819 as the date of building nos. 1-6.**

Incidentally, this phasing explains why the drains from no.21 (and correspondingly no.6 at the inner end of the next section to be built) run from the back of the house right through to connect with the main pipes at the front under Marshall Place, while all those adjoining run directly out to the back lane.

But for many years even these few would not sell. While making full allowance for adverse economic conditions, potential demand had been wildly exaggerated. What a sad end to the magnificent vision of the four residential squares! And what a disappointment to Robert Reid, whose first scheme had been abandoned and yet whose second, far more economical scheme couldn't get off the ground either! Perth was not Edinburgh. Inevitably, the plan also shows incongruous buildings already appearing behind on William Street.

1822 marked the celebrated visit to Edinburgh of King George IV accompanied by the Home Secretary, Robert Peel. In charge of the arrangements was Walter Scott himself. But the celebrations were cut short by news of the suicide of the Foreign Secretary, Lord Castlereagh, who had slit his throat with a letter opener, apparently for fear of exposure or blackmail because of his homosexual behaviour. By the way, the King's yacht, moored in the Forth, was the *'Royal George'*, which is the name of the grandest hotel in Perth.

Then the stock market crash of 1825 created fresh financial difficulties. It contributed to Sir Walter Scott's downfall and ruined scores of lesser Scottish notables. Reference must be made here to the first publication of *'St Valentine's Day, or The Fair Maid of Perth'* in 1828, coinciding with Scott's last visit to the city. He arrived from London via Edinburgh and Fife, making the last leg of the journey by boat from Dundee. He wrote: *"We landed on the South Inch, opposite the Hill of Kinnoul."*

(Scott, by the way, was born in 1771, just one year after Marshall and three years before Reid. 1808, when Marshall died and those first 8 houses in Marshall Place were built, saw publication of *'Marmion'*.)

Unsurprisingly, the plans dated **1829** for the proposed Water Works and those of **1832** by respectively the Edinburgh lithographer W. Banks and J Gardner of London, all show no change on Marshall Place. The 1832 Plan was one sheet in a superb volume (kept in one of Edinburgh Central Public Library's special collections) published in association with the Reform Act and entitled: "Plans of the Cities, Burghs and Boroughs of Scotland and Ireland as established by the respective Acts passed 7 July and 7 August 1832". It clearly shows just the 8 houses at the West end and 6 at the East – but, curiously, on "Marshall *Street*".

By 1832 (the year, too, of Walter Scott's death), those first eight houses (nos. 21-28) had already stood alone for some twenty-four years. But that lamentable situation persisted for only one more year. A plan produced by Leslie's Perth Directory of 1837-38 depicting both terraces completed – as does a pictorial plan published by J & D Nichol of Montrose of about the same year.

**After a quarter-century of stagnation, conditions must have improved dramatically to justify construction of the remaining fourteen houses in 1832-33 – just too late for revision of Gardner's Town Plan which had already gone for engraving.**

There was indeed a remarkable economic boom from 1830 onwards, with the foundation of the Perth Harbour Commission, dredging the river to take larger vessels and enlarging the docks and ship-building yards, as well as construction of the magnificent Waterworks (now the J D Fergusson art gallery) in 1831-34 on the corner of Marshall Place and Tay Street, which gave Perth its first supply of clean drinking water. Based on a new steam-pumping system, this was the product of an unsung mechanical genius, Adam Anderson (1780-1846), who had already designed and supervised the installation of the town's first gas supply in 1824 – and all as an amateur engineer, in his spare time, while Rector of the new Perth Academy from 1809 to 1837.

The Reform Act of 1832 also gave great impetus to this revival of prosperity. Then the County & City Infirmary, in York Place, opened in 1836. Three new flax spinning mills were founded in this decade. The Perth Banking Company (of which Thomas Anderson and his son-in-law Thomas Hay Marshall had been successively President) was relaunched, issuing its own notes. The enlarged Salutation Hotel opened in 1831, the year of a national census, showing a sudden growth in the town's population.

Among the symptoms of euphoria in this heady era, the beautiful painting of c.1831 by William Brown, 'Perth from Barnhill' *[page 26]* prominently prefigures Marshall Place with not only the two familiar terraces but two more again, identically, filling the frontages of the two blocks west of Scott Street. This was indeed a serious proposal, not merely artistic licence. Moreover, it was good planning, for the third terrace would have extended to James Street and the final one to King Street, i.e. the southern continuation of Methven Street which had been formed across the Hospital grounds (courtesy of Charles Archer) thereby completing the Canal Street–Methven/King Street–Marshall Place–Princes Street 'box'.

We know that Marshall Place was fully occupied by 1836 at the latest because the **1837** map was published to mark the launch of Leslie's annual 'Perth Directory'. The whole series is housed in the Local Studies Department of the A K Bell Library. Here is a list of the residents from that first issue. Note the houses' new street numbers.

| | | | |
|---|---|---|---|
| 1 | Archibald Reid, City Clerk | 15 | David Stuart, Grocer & Alexander Matthew "of customs" |
| 2 | Mrs Drummond | | |
| 3 | Wm Sandeman, Tea Merchant | 16 | Dr (Mrs) Ross |
| 4 | Mrs McFarlane | 17 | David Miller of Pow |

"Perth from Barnhill" (*detail*), by William Brown (c.1831)

| | | | |
|---|---|---|---|
| 5 | T R Sandeman | 18 | Mrs Laurence Robertson |
| | (but could have been 9 or 11) | 19 | Miss Riach |
| 6 | John Stewart, late Banker | 20 | Walter Miller of Perth Bank |
| 7 | Miss Sandeman & Mrs Gray | 21 | William Gloag, Banker |
| 8 | Mrs McLeod, Lodgings | 22 | James Rollo, Land Surveyor |
| 9 | | 23 | Patrick Soutar, Depute Sheriff-Clerk |
| 10 | Lt.Col. Balmain* | 24 | Miss Bisset** |
| 11 | | 25 | Mrs McVicar |
| 12 | John Flockhart, Writer | 26 | William & Peter Arnott |
| 13 | Mrs Matthew | 27 | John Stewart junior |
| 14 | Hugh Barclay, Sheriff-Substitute | 28 | John Johnston |

*Some thirty years earlier, one James Balmain had been Inspector of Public Works – an office commonly recruited from the military.

**A document in the National Archives dated 5 November 1829 refers to "Commissary General J Bisset" at No.5 Marshall Place, so maybe he had died before 1837; or else he was still there, with Miss Bisset (his sister?) at No.24 and T R Sandeman at 9 or 11?

The railway age arrived with the Perth-Dundee line in 1848, which had to be constructed along a massive high wall immediately behind Marshall Place (level with my second-floor study window, 30 yards Northwards) in order to maintain sufficient height to bridge over the several northbound streets and, particularly, over the River Tay. That, of course, finally destroyed any vestige of Reid's grand design, isolating Marshall Place from its urban hinterland, but conversely binding it even more closely to the South Inch.

Papers dated 1845-51 relating to the Dundee and Perth Railway Company's projected bridge across the Tay at Perth include this from 1847:

*"Copy of report and claim by Messrs [Robert] Stevenson, Civil Engineers, Edinburgh, to the magistrates and harbour commissioners of Perth relating to the agreement of the Dundee and Perth Railway Company to adopt the proposed line along the back of Marshall Place…as the attempt to intrude upon and destroy the Inch having been foiled by the exertions of the Town of Perth, and the site for the terminus being now it is believed finally fixed at the northern side of the suburb of St Leonards…and to the proposals of the Dundee and Perth [later the Aberdeen and Perth] Railway Company to dispense altogether with a drawbridge and instead to erect a bridge across the Tay with two arches each of 150 feet span and to pay the sum of £1,000 in consideration of the saving which they would effect if allowed to cross the river by a bridge on such a plan."*

The Stevensons were a great engineering dynasty, chiefly renowned for the building of lighthouses. One member of the next generation, Robert Louis, first entered the family firm before transferring to the study of law which he then abandoned in favour of writing. Incidentally, it is evident from that tribute demanded by the Town that the present-day practice of 'Planning Gain' – the extraction by Councils of capital contributions from developers, for unrelated civic improvements or purely for revenue, as the *quid pro quo* for the grant of a planning consent – is nothing new!

The attraction of the St. Leonards site was its elevation, at the height required to carry the Dundee-Aberdeen line, via a high wall behind Marshall Place, across a bridge over the Tay. But in 1850 Perth Town Council presented a claim for compensation arising from this very costly form of construction (which incidentally destroyed the original mews behind the two terraces, although still leaving a perfectly adequate lane for rear access).

For this had indeed been a battle between the Town and the Railway Company, who had fiercely pursued plans to locate the Station actually on the South Inch, closer to The Shore (docks) and the city centre. The Council had to petition the House of Commons in opposition to the Dundee and Perth Extension Bill of 1847 and even went to court in 1849 to raise an interdict (injunction).

It was, however, the rival Scottish Central Railway Company that promoted the successful campaign to site the terminus at the west end of the town. The Dundee and Perth Railway Company nevertheless established the Princes Street Station, between the Waterworks and Greyfriars Cemetery, but that closed following the inevitable centralization at St Leonards.

J D Fergusson art gallery, Perth.

# Chapter III

## COUNCIL MINUTES
### – *the municipal plot*

The last Chapter's historical background will have illuminated the following excerpts from the Council Minutes, with special reference to the evolution of Marshall Place and the fates of its promoters.

**3 May 1802**:   "The Council authorize the Magistrates to cause to make a plan of the ground at the South end *[sic: 'North' was meant – how curious that the item introducing this proposal contains such a cardinal error – but it was a late item added to an already exhausting agenda]* of the South Inch and west side of the Turnpike *[the Edinburgh road]* with the plan and section of a row of houses intended to be built there and authorize the Chamberlain to pay the expense thereof not to exceed ten guineas."

**7 June 1802**:   "The Provost reported that as authorised by Act of Council of Third May last, he had caused Mr Robert Reid Architect in Edinburgh make plans of the front elevations and ground plan and section of the intended buildings upon the ground proposed to be feued at the North end of the South Inch, and which he now laid before the Council which being considered by the Council they appointed the Magistrates late Provost Black Bailie Proudfoot Bailie McEwan Baillie Scott Convener Muir and Deacon Square as a Committee for considering the said plans and proposed measure and to report."

But the Magistrates had been given no more authority than to have a plan of the ground prepared, yet the Provost, Thomas Hay Marshall, who was, significantly, near the end of his first two-year term of office, had taken it upon himself to commission Robert Reid to proceed with the project.  Moreover, Marshall and Reid were so confident of approval that, despite the difficulties of remote communication and travel between Perth and Edinburgh, Reid could instantly agree terms of appointment, plan the work, conduct his surveys and inquiries and produce finished drawings – all within one month, which was simply not possible!

So that item must indeed have been hurriedly raised at close of business on 3 May (hence the clerical error) **after** Reid had already been promised the job by his all-powerful friend the

Provost – and, indeed, after he had already got on with it. We know from Buist's 1787 town plan that development along this east-west line had long been mooted, so Marshall and Reid had been privately working on it for a while.

Marshall had succeeded Thomas Black as Provost on 29 September 1800, and was re-elected in 1801. In 1802 he was succeeded by John Caw who in turn was re-elected in 1803, only to be succeeded in 1804 again by Marshall who was re-elected – for a fourth term – on 30 September 1805. That was three weeks before the Battle of Trafalgar; hence the name of Nelson Street eventually given to the side-street between the two terraces. On 29 September 1806 he was finally succeeded once more by John Caw – who was likewise re-elected for a fourth term in 1807.

So those two between them led the City and Royal Burgh for the first eight years of the century. Incidentally, although the Scottish law-term days fell in May (Whitsun), August (Lammas), November (Martinmas) and February (Candlemas), the municipal elections were held around the English quarter-day of Michaelmas (29 September), which also marked the end of the financial year, and had done so since the Reformation.

This cosy convention of alternating at two-yearly intervals arose after 11 October 1676 when the Council resolved: "for avoiding the great confusion still threatening…That in all time coming, no Provost, Dean of Guild or Bailie shall continue any longer in the said offices than for two years together" – but there was nothing to prevent their taking turn about! The upheavals following restoration of the monarchy in 1660, while local government was still torn between Cromwellians and royalists, were exploited for nepotistic and other corrupt purposes. One Patrick Threipland had been Provost for eleven years – continuously since 1664 apart from the year 1670 when (owing to some domestic circumstance) it suited him to substitute George Threipland – until his regime faltered when in the elections of 4 October 1675 he was supplanted by one Archibald Chrystie, but only until the following 16 March when, in mid-term, "By a Warrand from the Lords of Secret Council" – an exceptional and highly irregular procedure – he succeeded in ousting the incumbent and reinstating himself. Not only that; he made sure of the right result when the next elections were held six months later.

But he had gone too far – hence the Council's extraordinary resolution on 11 October. A week later, on 18 October, the Council sent a senior Bailie "to repair to Edinburgh, and give a true account to the Lords of Privy Seal, and other persons of quality, of the form and manner of the last election, that the misrepresentation of Sir Patrick Threipland, late Provost, may not harbour with them as truth" *(James Cant)*.

Consequently, on 11 November 1676, there was a thorough purge and new Councillors were chosen, and "the whole Council swore not to vote for the continuance of the Magistrates above two years."

Reid's task of undertaking the design of the proposed houses at extremely short notice was admittedly eased by his concurrent involvement in Perth on Marshall's behalf, as already evidenced only a few months earlier, by a Minute of the Meeting on **4 January 1802:**

"Provost Marshall stated to the Council that it had been sometime ago under consideration to erect a Building sufficient to contain the whole Seminaries and with this view the Draught of a Building had been prepared by Mr Reid Architect in Edinburgh which was shown to the Council. And the Provost made offer to the Council of ground sufficient for that Building agreeable to that plan on Rose Terrace being ninety feet in front…"

So here was Provost Marshall informing the Council what, according to him, they had had under consideration for some while – yet with no reference to any previous Meeting! Moreover, he again did so having already, without authority, commissioned Reid to produce this plan for the building, of what became Perth Academy, on land that he himself owned, and which he presented the Council as a fait accompli! This was not purely philanthropic, for while he appears to have donated the land, it was part of the much larger scheme. Naturally, approval was readily granted. (Society had not yet conceived the notion of 'conflict of interest', but we must not judge standards of public or political morality of that robust, expansionist era by those of our own envious, repressive age.)

The Register of Sasines duly records that the sale by Marshall to 'The Magistrates' of the site for the school building was not completed until 22 February 1804 – more than two years after the Council had approved the proposal! Raising the funds and building were bound to take a long time, but that was of no consequence to Marshall and Reid's strategy: all that mattered was securing the consent. Among papers belonging to the Town, now in Perth Archives (B59/24/1/109), which were found in the office of the late William Stewart, Writer (i.e. Writer to the Signet – solicitor) of Perth – of whom we shall hear much more later – was the Feu Charter dated 7 October 1803 and Instrument of Sasine registered 25 February 1804.

The list of subscriptions for building the Seminaries (1804-05) includes "Thomas Hay-Marshall, the ground upon which the building is to be erected, value £500" (c.£100,000 today), but of course that was not cash but merely a notional and perhaps inflated valuation. He has another entry, too, as "Lieut.Col. Marshall, the surplus fund of the 2nd Battalion of Royal Perth Volunteers, £400" – this, as mentioned earlier, was the officers' back pay which they never drawn but left to accumulate in a 'contingency fund', not knowing how long the national emergency might last or whether financial support might have been wanted for families of any casualties.

This list also includes donations from all the principals involved in the Marshall Place project ("the usual suspects") William Stewart, Writer, Robert Peddie, Writer (and Town Clerk) and George Condie, Writer – these three handled all the legal and financial work – Bailie John McEwan, mason, Charles Archer, merchant; ex-Provost James Ramsay; William Marshall, agent for the Bank of Scotland; William Gray, ironmonger; Alexander Paul, merchant, and Robert

Reid himself: but none of those who (as we shall see later) won in the end – Messrs Gloag, Morton and Greig.

We already know that James Ramsay (Provost 1794-96) was founder of the local militia and, as we shall see, also one of the original feuars of Marshall Place and a partner of Thomas Anderson in the Town's Mills, so it was true to form that in 1815 his daughter Agnes married the brilliant young Rector of the Academy, Adam Anderson.

Incidentally, this new Academy struggled to retain staff in its early years, because of the troubled times and because it was never adequately endowed. I cannot resist digressing, to publish a letter found in the City Archives (PE15) from one W D Russel, a French teacher, informing his landlord in Rose Terrace, one Robert Hepburn, that he will be

*"forced to leave your tenement unless effectual means be taken to put an end to the acts of malignity and party spirit which I have daily experienced ever since I commenced my course of lectures….it is clearly perceptible that the anxious desire of annoying me pervades the breast of every youth whether male or female that attends the Grammar School and Academy; it cannot be otherwise whereas they have imbibed this propensity from some of their unmanly and ungenerous masters."*

But the founding of the Seminaries demonstrated the power of Marshall as well as his close relationship with Reid. Indeed, Reid had been working on Rose Terrace since 1797, when Reid was aged only 23. (As we have seen, the Seminaries was already illustrated on Kirkwood's 1805 Town Map.) And he was working on Atholl Street (& Bridge Street) 1806-09, before and after his master's death.

Furthermore, those same Minutes of **7 June 1802** refer to a plan showing that: "the street named Methven Street is to be continued and extended through the hospital grounds southward (what became King Street) til it join the road proposed to be made in the South Inch as marked on said plan" and they also incorporate this letter from "**Charles Archer** Merchant in Perth:"

*"Gentlemen 5th June 1802 – I have seen the plan for the continuation of Methven Street thro' the hospital ground, for enlarging the South Inch and opening several streets…one of which is to run thro' the property lately purchased by me from Capt. Wood [presumably the same 'Mr Wood' shown on Buist's 1787 plan as owner of the extensive 'Spey Gardens' to the West of Gray Friars]. Being fully persuaded that this measure if carried into effect will not only prove highly ornamental to the Town but be advantageous for all concerned, the plan has my hearty approbation. If any more formal obligation to conform to it than this letter is necessary on my part I am ready to grant it. (signed) Charles Archer.'"*

The ground to be acquired at the foot of Methven Street belonged to the King James VI Hospital which had been built fifty years earlier, on the site of the former Charterhouse, Scotland's only Carthusian Priory.

The new road scheme was, as usual, instantly and unanimously approved. So (a) Archer happened to acquire the land shortly before this profitable new road scheme was announced, (b) his letter was dated two days before the Council Meeting, and (c) by then, although not a Councillor, he had already had a preview of the plans – a fact which he was happy to declare officially! But once again, the conduct of Marshall and Archer was so transparent that no question of culpability arose; for those in authority unashamedly enjoyed its exercise and the opportunities it afforded, to get things done incredibly quickly for the whole Town's benefit as well as, occasionally, for their own.

Consequently, at that one Council Meeting, plans were presented and approved for both the Marshall Place development and the new King Street to connect with its west end…...all without any prior discussion or authority!

Captain Charles Archer, of course, was a fellow-officer in the Volunteers. There can be no doubt that promotion of both the Marshall Place and King Street projects was coordinated. There was no question of having to wait for approval of Robert Reid's scheme for a new housing development along the proposed new East-West road before submitting a plan for a new North-South road which depended on it.

For by now the Marshall-Reid vehicle was in over-drive. With barely three months left before the Elections when he would have to stand down, Marshall convened another Council Meeting just one week later, on **14 June 1802**, at which it was minuted that:

"The Committee appointed on the Seventh current relative to the intended feus at the South Inch reported that they had considered the plans prepared by Mr Reid Architect laid before them and approved thereof and were of opinion that the purchasers of the respective Lots should be bound to erect thereon Buildings conform to the plans at least in front roofs and gavels the front to be of ashlar work and not to be more than two feet longer or any shorter than the dimensions on the plans. That the purchasers should be taken bound to inclose their Lots with walls and iron railings as aftermentioned, the divisions betwixt the Lots to be built and made mutually by the contiguous proprietors and that within twelve months after Martinmas next the front railing and wall to be of the dimensions on the plan No.1 the divisions between the Lots from the front railing as far north as the front walls of the houses to consist of a wall the same dimensions and railing And a like wall and rail to run east and west in a line with the front walls of the houses – That no other buildings should be erected on the said ground to the south of the line of the back walls of the houses higher than the wall of said railing to run east and west – And that the divisions betwixt the Lots to the north of the houses be not less than nine feet above the surface of the ground.

(*These were obviously intended to be most imposing residences, with walls dividing the back gardens at least nine feet high!*)

The Committee were further of opinion that the said Lots of ground should immediately be brought into the market and exposed in seven Lots at two hundred pounds of upsett price each and four pounds each of yearly feu duty And that in said feus the Town should restrict themselves from erecting any buildings on the South Inch in front of said Lots of ground within four hundred yards of the front wall and railing thereof. Of which report the Council approve and authorise the Magistrates to cause straight the line of march *[boundary]* betwixt the Town's property and **Captain Archer**'s by giving and taking ground in equal quantities And resolve the said march being so straightened that a street along the said march be made of twentyfive feet in breadth, towards which street the said **Charles Archer** shall give ten feet of his property disponing the same to the Town, the Town giving the other fifteen feet off their ground – and said marches being so settled and the street lined off recommend to the Magistrates to cause rutt out on the ground the several Lots to be exposed to public roup within the Town House upon Friday twentyfifth current at twelve noon and to be advertised thro' the town by the Bell or Drum *[i.e. by the Crier]* & in the Edinburgh papers and empower the Magistrates to settle with the Inch Masters & report, and also to prepare articles of roup."

*Note Archer's inevitable involvement, and the terms of the land-swap ('excambion') at 15 to 10 in his favour!*

**Thus, a mere seven days after the Council's first sight of Robert Reid's design for the proposed development and appointment of a Committee to study it, the Council was able to determine not only the detailed specification for the houses but also plans for the new road and the terms of sale of the individual lots by auction which was to be held only eleven days later!**

**Such a whirlwind programme was not only totally unjustified but physically impossible. It could be achieved only if a clique of the Council had been given a free hand and had prepared well in advance. To conclude the transaction for exchange of land with Charles Archer, plan the new road, prepare Articles of Roup** (*auction particulars*)**, advertise in the Edinburgh papers and organize the sale in the Town House, could not all have been accomplished within eleven days – more like eleven weeks would normally have been required. Any interested members of the public were given practically no notice or opportunity of taking part. It was all planned and progressed behind the scenes.**

The City Archives hold the original Articles of Roup, dated 25 June 1802, as directed by that Council Minute of 14 June. So these essential terms and conditions were produced only on the morning of the auction at 12 noon.

The Councillors authorizing the proceedings included Thomas Hay Marshall (present Provost), Peter Duff (present Dean of Guild), John Caw (next Provost), William Blair (Town Treasurer) and three other Bailies. The presiding officer ('Judge') was John Gloag, scion of another Perth dynasty. The exceptional importance of the project to those concerned is reflected in this galaxy of sponsors – Perth's *crème de la crème*.

The accompanying report on the Roup identifies the prices paid, the purchasers and their 'Cautioners' (i.e. sureties or guarantors) as follows:

| Lot | Price | Purchaser | Cautioner |
|-----|-------|-----------|-----------|
| One | £200 | Bailie John McEwan | Thomas Hay Marshall |
| Three | £200 | Alexander Paul | Patrick Stewart |
| Four | £200 | James Ramsay (past Provost) | George Ramsay |
| Five | £200 | William Marshall | Charles Archer |
| Seven | £261 | John McEwan | Thomas Hay Marshall |

Thus, in four of the five cases, only the bare upset price (reserve) needed to be paid. So there were no competing bids at all. A higher price had to be paid only for Lot Seven, which was worth more because (i) it was on the most prominent corner facing the Edinburgh Turnpike and (ii) it included an extension on the Princes Street return frontage, just as Lot One included an extension up the future Scott Street – both being acquired by the Senior Bailie who also happened to have been a member of the committee set up to plan the whole project. Furthermore, there were no bids at all for Lots Two and Six. The question arises: was anybody else present?

There had to be one, at least – Alexander Paul – the only one of the four purchasers who was not a member of the 'Magic Circle'. But the others made short work of him, as we shall see. Incidentally, William Marshall (no relation) was Agent for the Bank of Scotland and therefore *persona grata*.

Meanwhile, maintaining the momentum, the Council's next meeting was held only ten days after the sale, on **5 July 1802**, at which the transactions were ratified – sustaining the frantic rush. The clerks must have been writing furiously, to produce the five complex feu charters (complete with building specifications) within barely a week. The only excuse for proceeding in such a headlong fashion was that it succeeded – or, rather, they thought it had!

They would have been well advised to proceed much more cautiously, since what was eventually built and is today – two centuries later – enjoying such a revival of interest and extensive restoration, bears no resemblance to Reid's original design for seven villas. As we shall see, *hubris* was quickly followed by *nemesis*.

The Council planned and promoted the design and development of a mere seven houses as a major civic enterprise, risking public money in assembling the land, planning the new public road and auctioning the feus – an absurdly over-ambitious scheme undertaken in the most unseemly haste – and solely for the benefit of a handful of the civic leaders.

While the design of the houses was highly specified, no descriptions or dimensions of the Lots were given, except by reference to Buist's survey of 1787 and to Reid's plans, which do not appear to have survived.

## Lot Second

Bailie McEwan's offer for Lot Seventh, after he had already acquired Lot First at the bare 'upsett price' (reserve) happened, naturally, to be the 'last and highest' offer. A late addition to these Minutes also records that an offer had been received for Lot Second at the upset price of £200 from William Stewart, Writer and brother-officer in the militia, in the form of a simple letter, dated 26 June 1802, addressed to Provost Marshall personally, and nominating Charles Archer and David Walker as his Cautioners; which was accepted on 5 July. William Stewart, of course, was Bailie McEwan's solicitor; but since McEwan had just picked up the second last Lot, it looked better that his nominee collected the very last.

**It was therefore not surprising that the original Articles of Roup and associated records are among the catalogued papers found by Robert Peddie (Town Clerk) in William Stewart's office upon his death in 1813.**

**11 October 1802**   "The Council appoint as a Committee relative to the new buildings at South Inch and improvements there – Thomas Black and Thomas Hay Marshall late Provosts, James Proudfoot John McEwan *(the purchaser of Lots no.1 & 7!)* and John Scott late Bailies, James Scott Deacon of Wrights, William Square Deacon of Hammermen, along with the present Magistrates."

Marshall no doubt agreed to serve because he had just ended his first two-year term as Provost and because he had no direct financial stake in the enterprise.

But why bother to form a high-powered Committee, just to oversee the development of seven houses, on plots of which two had already been acquired by one Member of that Committee and one more by another?  Why, other than to ensure that everything possible was done in the name of the Councillors to promote their own interests?  In any event, there is no record that this 'camouflage' Committee ever reported or even met again.

Among such graphic entries as one appearing in a prominent citizen's account for a sum due to "Aliment for his wife's idiot bastard", the Town Chamberlain's Accounts for the year 1801-1802 show, in an addendum, under 'Additional Revenue' due in the next year (payable at Martinmas 1803): sums of £200 for purchase of South Inch Lots and £4 feu duties in respect of nos. 1,2,3, &,5 (but not no.6) and £261 purchase plus £4 feu for no. 7.  Yet the Accounts for 1802-1803 record that those feu duties due on 12 November 1803 all remained unpaid at 31 December!

*"South Inch Lots: John McEwan  £12; Alexr. Paul £4; James Ramsay £4; Wm. Stewart  £4"* Also duly recorded, under 'Sales of Town's Property': *"South Inch Lots   £1,061."*

But that accounts for only five out of the six sold, because Alexr. Paul's purchase price of £200 was recorded as still not paid.  The Accounts for the next year (03-04) show the same overdue payments for feu duties, except that Alexr. Paul is now debited with £8 for two Lots. So more than two years after the Council, on 5th July 1802, authorized acceptance of the offers for the feus from these civic dignitaries, they have still not paid.  These eminent citizens were flagrant defaulters, yet evidently immune to penalty.

**6 June 1803**   (following an agreement with a contractor for deepening a water-course on the West side of the South Inch and disposing of the spoil):

"that as the proprietors of Marshall Place *[already the new road has been named after the past & future Provost, even though it had not yet been constructed]* had occasion for a considerable quantity of forced Earth in execution of the plan laid down for their buildings there, they had made offer of the following sums for filling up the forty feet in front of their Lots to the average depth of two & a half feet: late Provost Ramsay five pounds Bailie McEwan eight pounds Mr William Stewart four pounds & **Mr Alexander Paul** four pounds and which offer the Provost in names of the Magistrates had accepted and the Council approve thereof."

Though seemingly trivial, this was an important matter to the eminent feuars – who were careful to have themselves represented in the Council Minutes as "the proprietors of Marshall Place", even though they had not yet paid for the feus!  But it was important, too, because the reason for spending so much was to raise the level of the front gardens as a protection against flooding from the River Tay. *(See Professor Walker's comment in Appendix 'A'.)*

But otherwise, dead silence prevailed throughout 1803.

**6 February 1804**   "The Council agree to make the roads upon the North and South sides of the Lots on Marshall Place when necessary, that on the Northside to be twentyfive feet in breadth and that on the Southside forty feet in breadth as mentioned in the articles of roup and laid down on the plan therein referred to."   Note the grudging "when necessary".

The Council was half-heartedly undertaking to form these two roads, just to serve seven houses, even though there was no sign that they would ever be built.   Pressure was growing on the purchasers to pay up and start building, and on the Council to provide what in modern jargon we would call infrastructure and environmental improvements.

**5 March 1804**   "Upon an application of Bailie John McEwan stating that he had purchased from Mr William Marshall, Agent for the Bank of Scotland, that Lot being Number Fifth at Marshall Place which was sold by the Town to him at the public roup upon the 25th *[unusually in numerals]* of June 1802 – And craved that the Charter thereof should be granted in his favour.   The Council agree to the said request and authorize ….."

But he had actually arranged to acquire this Lot some fourteen months earlier.   For in the City Archives is the following letter [PE16 Bundle 34] written by William Marshall to Bailie John McEwan dated November 1802:

## *Lot Fifth*

"Sir, I hereby make over and give up to you that feu of ground on the South Inch of Perth being the third Lot counting from the road to the South *[i.e. from E to W, but Lot Fifth, reading from W to E as originally numbered]* feued by and from the Town of Perth and I authorize you to apply for and obtain the same to be disponed to you upon condition that you shall pay and perform everything that I engaged to pay and perform by the Minute of Sale and premium entered into and between me and the Town of Perth subject to the Articles of Roup of the said and other Lots as concerned and relating to these Articles.   I am Sir, William Marshall."

Why the delay?   It cannot have been in order to force a reduction in terms, since Marshall was clearly making nothing out of it:   he was simply handing it over on the same terms.   No doubt McEwan was simply holding off until he knew that the roads were going through.   But why should he, having already acquired Lots First and Seventh, acquire Lot Fifth as well?

As a master mason and building contractor, was he simply increasing his turnover, or was he speculating that, once developed, the houses could be sold at a worth-while profit: surely a risky business with no evidence of demand and in the midst of War – with its desperate shortages of timber and other building materials and labour, not to mention working capital? George Penny's 'Traditions of Perth' records that Bailie McEwan had "built the Horse Barracks and St Paul's Church, and erected several houses in John Street and on the west side of St Paul's Church, and also a number in Marshall Place" (but later, of course).

Yet otherwise, the dead silence continued throughout 1804. Since no real progress was made during that year-and-three-quarters, the frantic rush in the Spring and Summer of 1802 was all the more culpable. No wonder nothing more was ever heard of that Committee appointed in October 1802!

## Lot Sixth

At last, the remaining Lot was sold by Public Roup on 1st February 1805, to Bailie McEwan, at a price of £150 – a reduction of one quarter – two-and-a-half years after the original sales, throughout which there had been no demand. They must all have been getting very worried! By the way, the Judge at that Roup was David George Sandeman (of course!), not that much judgment was necessary, since there cannot have been any other bids.

So suddenly, but not surprisingly, we find this Minute of the Council Meeting on **6 January 1806:**

"A petition and memorial of the proprietors of Marshall Place, stating that finding the former plan for building there would be attended with so much expense as to prove a very losing concern to the purchasers, they had applied to Mr Reid the Architect to draw out another plan so as to be equally elegant in its appearance and at the same time to contain more accommodation, which plan along with Mr Reid's observations they hoped would be approved of as much superior to the other and would also ensure the same being immediately carried into execution. Being read and the same together with the plan and observations by Mr Reid taken into consideration, the Council upon condition that the whole houses upon Marshall Place shall be built agreeable to the present plan within eight years after Whitsunday next under the penalty of paying double feu duty for such Lots as may not then be built in all time thereafter and proportionally *for any space less than a Lot [my emphasis]* and that the proprietors be bound to adhere to working drawings to be furnished by Mr Reid the Architect who made the plan and that the fronts of the houses to be all built of stone of the same colour and the houses built in every respect exactly conform to the plan now produced, now agree to adopt that plan in place of the former one declaring expressly that the whole other obligations in the Charters under which the Lots of Marshall Place were feued shall be adhered to. The plan was subscribed by the Provost in face of Council."

Perplexingly, there is no reference to the disruption of the original plans caused by the insertion of Nelson Street, which must have been planned by now. This disruption explains the reason for the added qualification: "….and proportionally for any space less than a Lot".

That they were given another eight years – i.e. until May 1814 – shows the extremity of the crisis confronting them, not only on account of the very difficult economic conditions prevailing but more particularly because of the hopeless non-viability of the original scheme. In any event, those illustrious citizens needed this long-term rescue package. The very next item in the same Minutes is highly illuminating.

*"Bailie McEwan agrees to take the Lot in Marshall Place still belonging to the Town at two hundred pounds sterling of price and four pounds sterling of yearly feu duty, the price and first year's feu duty being payable at Martinmas next eighteen hundred and six and to be liable…"*

But hadn't he already bought it for only £150 at auction eleven months ago; or had he defaulted, choosing not to settle but to hang on until the new plan had been approved? Anyhow, McEwan, the speculative builder, now owned four Lots – his original First, to which he added Seventh, then took over Fifth from the Bank, and finally picks up Lot Sixth – four out of seven!

Why incur such heavy additional liabilities? Ah, but it is now a far different and much more economical scheme, consisting of 28 terraced houses instead of seven villas. But what was the precise extent of this Lot and, yet again, what was the formula for effecting the transformation? For this was the crucial juncture, immediately after the 'petition and memorial' was approved on such advantageous terms, whereupon McEwan snapped up the one remaining Lot.

Certainly, the circumstances of the transformation of the plans, by dictat of the Council, and instant sale of the last Lot to one of the Councillors, with no thought of re-advertising, provide final proof of complicity. As for the undertaking that the new scheme would "ensure the same being immediately carried into execution" – that was sheer effrontery.

The expression "still belonging to the Town" did confirm that the whole scheme was always confined to just this small enclave. But this was not a case of making a major civic project out of such a modest scheme, but *vice versa* – a potentially major civic design dwindling to a modest row of twin terraces. The vision of a Southern New Town was no more than a Marshall-Reid pipe-dream. Then a real and costly disappointment was the failure of the plans whose purpose was to provide civic leaders with the exclusive opportunity either to build imposing villas for themselves in a glorious setting or to speculate in their development. But the final disappointment was the painful discovery that even the much reduced scheme would prove financially disastrous and take another 27 years to finish.

Yet much of Reid's original scheme survived elsewhere. For before Marshall Place was completed, plans were under way to build an amended form of those seven large villas nearby on St Leonard's Bank. As depicted in Macneil Macleay's painting *[page 12]*, they originally faced East, with magnificent front gardens running down to the South Inch, their gates opening onto a tree-lined avenue off Marshall Place and rear access from St Leonard's Bank. But after the Railway Station was built they were reversed, the avenue closed and absorbed into the Inch, leaving the villas with unattractive frontages to St Leonard's Bank but handsome backs and pedestrian gates onto the Inch, where the lines of trees are still discernible.

**28 March 1806** "The Council authorizes the Magistrates to cause make and finish the road in front of Marshall Place."

So authorization was hastily given for construction of the new road – two years after the Council had given approval to its formation and nearly four years after the Lots were sold – but within three months of the Council's consent to the new architectural concept. So why, at the outset, had there been such a frantic rush to commission and approve the original scheme and to lay out and dispose of the Lots? It can only have been to ensure that the local establishment kept tight control of the project. But as amateurs they could not see that such a precipitate start was bound to be followed by years of inactivity, which in turn would be followed by the discovery that the plans had to be scrapped and replaced by a completely different solution.

There is still no mention whatever of the decision to split the whole site on either side of a new road to be called Nelson Street, nor of the consequential effects on ownership of the seven Lots. The scheme for the creation of Nelson Street was the key to the whole new strategy, but known only to the conspirators themselves and remains a mystery today.

The City Archives reveal on one scrap of paper (PE15 Bundle 11) the "Estimates for construction of road in front of Marshall Place, dated 25 July 1807". By this late date, nos. 21-28 were actually under construction, yet still no road…..sixteen months' delay between authorization and obtaining cost estimates! That indicates even more clearly how precarious the project had become. What a contrast to the alacrity with which they had hurled themselves into it five years earlier! Only two contractors priced the job: James McDonald £256.10.0 and McLean whose first estimate of £154 on 23 July was increased the next day to £195 and accepted the day after – from which it is not difficult to deduce what happened behind the scenes! This resolution was added: "The Magistrates agree to make the above road by days' wages and empower Mr Alexander *(Master of Works)* to employ them to do the work on the best terms he can." Both employer and contractor must have become desperate.

Judging by the frequent items in the Minutes dealing with ways and means devised by the Council to raise additional funds, which seems to have been a constant preoccupation, the Council certainly needed the cash. At first, the idea of creating a site for a housing development of the highest quality, on virgin land which the Town already owned, by simply slicing a strip off the Northern side of the South Inch, no doubt presented an opportunity, which they seized upon urgently, to collect several grassums of £200 or more, as well as many years of advance feu duties, although what sums due were actually paid remains doubtful.

But in any event, how did they ever expect to sell an isolated parade of seven great houses, standing in a wilderness? This élite group of former Provosts and officers in the militia were never motivated by civic altruism: the entire venture seems a contrivance for private gain that proved completely misguided. From a traffic point of view, the road was not needed urgently, if at all; although no doubt the consensus was that – like Archer's commendation of the plan for King Street – it would be 'highly ornamental to the Town' and 'advantageous to all concerned' (or so they hoped), but that is scarcely a reason for a major road proposal.

Nor was there a conspicuous demand for new housing at this top end of the market. On the contrary, there was little or none: hence the period of 3½ years that elapsed between Bailie McEwan's purchases of Lots First and Sixth; and hence the same interval between the original sales and the purchasers' representations to change the plans.

So what possessed these civic dignitaries to sink their money into the scheme? How did they, with no prior experience, imagine that such a gamble could ever succeed – such an upmarket housing development in a provincial town in war-time conditions? Were Marshall's colleagues beguiled by Edinburgh's New Town development and by Reid's renown? No wonder the Council exercised extreme latitude, but they never imagined that completion of the development might be delayed until 30 years after inception and almost as long after the original purchasers had paid the Council for delivery of enough earth to fill their front plots.

Whatever the original motives for the scheme and however it was presented, for the trifling amount yielded by seven units it scarcely seemed worth the bother. Applying an historic inflationary multiplier of (say) 200, the seven grassums (original purchase prices for the feus) would have produced a grand total of less than £300,000 in today's money, and even less after allowing for the heavy extra costs of providing roads, lighting, etc.

Besides, only those few like Ramsay and McEwan could, themselves, hope to some extent to control the course of events, or an entrepreneur like Charles Archer who acquired Lot Third from Alexander Paul, the original purchaser three years earlier *(see extracts from the Title Deeds to 21 Marshall Place below)* and Lot Four from James Ramsay. Charles Archer was clearly in league with McEwan (and with Reid as willing accomplice), since his deal with Alexander Paul clearly anticipated the petition to the Council for approval of the new scheme.

### Eureka!

Now, everything suddenly falls into place. The essential mystery is solved. Let us 'marshall' the evidence!

16 August 1805: Charles Archer acquires Lot Third from Alexander Paul and (shortly thereafter) Lot Fourth from ex-Provost Ramsay.

6 January 1806: Council grants petition to replace original scheme for seven large villas on a continuous frontage with new plans for two terraces, separated by Nelson Street (less than three months after Trafalgar), so the creation of this new thoroughfare – carved out of Lot Fourth – must have formed part of the new scheme.

28 March 1806: Council authorizes construction of the roadway on Marshall Place – for completion in late 1807, while Archer & McEwan were building the first block of houses (nos. 21-28).

11 August 1806: Archer acquires land extending from Canal Street through to (the future) Victoria Street, to build his grand villa, commanding the vista down Nelson Street to the South Inch.

Finally, 1809: Robert Reid's own Town Plan, showing 21-28 Marshall Place and Archer's villa completed.

So Captain Archer is revealed as the arch-manipulator and promoter of the new project, having stayed out of the initial scheme altogether (apart from participating profitably in the land assembly) and then picking up three of the seven Lots cheaply from the original purchasers. He does seem a most conceited fellow, with his mansion commanding a grand approach via the purpose-built Nelson Street, and the permanent title of "Captain", which was only a temporary rank in the militia and a fairly modest one, compared to his friends' 'Colonel', Major, etc.,

"The South Inch",  Painting by
Macneil Macleay (1842)

which they quickly discarded.  So he had master-minded the whole scheme, with Bailie McEwan as a willing accomplice and builder.  (Was Reid ever paid his fees for the abortive scheme or did he load them onto its replacement or simply write them off – or effectively recoup them from the lucrative Prison commission?)

But this was Captain Archer's zenith.  Nothing went right for him thereafter. Meanwhile, Marshall and Robert Reid were enjoying their heyday.

**29 September 1806**   The Council voted one hundred guineas (over £20,000 today) for a presentation of 'Plate' to Thomas Hay Marshall:

*"as a mark of the high sense they entertain of the services rendered by him to the Community by suggesting and promoting plans beneficial to the revenue and highly ornamental to the City…"*

**6 October 1806**   Provost Caw, past Provost Thomas Hay Marshall and Bailie Ross comprised a *"Committee relative to the new Prison and to matters connected therewith."*

Robert Reid was again handed this most desirable architectural commission, although it was as slow to get off the ground as Marshall Place, half a mile up the Edinburgh turnpike.  It was needed to accommodate 7,000 French prisoners-of-war, but was not built until 1810-12, after Marshall's death, having cost the enormous sum of £130,000, which proved a very poor investment.  Why the Ministers in London decided to spend so much public money on such a magnificent building merely to house French prisoners, and so far north of the theatre of war – and what, incidentally, became of the inmates on their eventual release – does not concern us here, but it was certainly another coup for the Perth economy, as well as for Marshall and Reid.   The structure principally comprised five three-storey halls set on a polygonal-ended base, but in 1839-42 was replaced, again at vast public expense, by Thomas Brown's more conventional radial design of four whinstone halls to provide Scotland's first general prison. However, the arcaded guardhouses fronting Edinburgh road, as well as much of North Square, the perimeter wall and canal survive from Reid's original scheme.

Incidentally, it was in 1807 that Perth was divided into four parishes, by designated the great St Jon's Kirk as comprising three churches – Middle, East and West – while a new church, St. Paul's, was built at the junction of High Street and Methven Street – Bailie McEwan once again the contractor.

Thomas Hay Marshall had persevered as a Councillor beyond the 1807 Elections, but his attendance at Council Meetings faltered, his last appearance (as noted earlier) being on 6 June 1808, barely a month before his death on 15 July.

The poor state of the Town's finances worsened.  A report to the Council Meeting on **5 June 1809**, reproduced accounts showing the year's Revenue as £4,688.8.10 (including 'Feu Duties & Ground Annuals' of £182.4.4) and Expenditure as £6,244.8.1 (including £1,745.16.0 as "Interest on borrowed money and annuities"), producing a huge deficit of £1,555.19.3.  So the income amounted to barely three-quarters of the expenditure, while the cost of interest on borrowed money plus the cost of annuities amounting to almost 28% of total expenditure – exceeding the deficit!

Incidentally, throughout this era more than one tenth of the Burgh's total income year by year derived from the sale of pews in its four churches. The only remedies that the Council could suggest was an increase in Shore Dues (on goods discharged at the docks) and introduction of assessments on all residents for paving and lighting the streets, to supplement the traditional local tax called 'Cess' – which was the forerunner of the rating system. A Minute dated **3 July 1815** reports on a letter, addressed to the Provost, from Mr David Black, Agent for the British Linen Company, demanding payment of the Town's Bond to that Company for five hundred pounds, in response to which the Bank is told it will have to wait: *"the Council are of opinion that application should be made to Mr Black for further indulgence in point of time for paying up that sum, which is inconvenient at present."*

In February 1810 John McEwan at last sold two of the houses he had built within Lot One, to William and Peter Arnot, each for £845.00, described as second and third tenements from the left; i.e. nos. 26 and 27. These buyers are still listed as owners of no.26 in Leslie's 1837 Directory.

**6 November 1810**    "The Council authorizes the Magistrates to cause place four or five lamps in the Street at Marshall Place and to settle with the Contractors for the expense…" All for the benefit of eight houses, some of which were not yet occupied.

In March 1815 Charles Archer sold to William Gloag for £970 one of the houses he had built within Lot Three – *see 'Title Deeds'* – but that, as we shall see, was an artificially inflated figure!

Transactions by Margaret Gray and Jean McEwan, daughters of Bailie McEwan who had meanwhile died, show that no.1 Marshall Place, the block on the corner of Princes Street – part of Lot Seven – was actually built on its own in 1815.

**So it was not the case, as assumed hitherto, that nos.1 to 6 were built as one section in 1819-20, but rather that nos.2 to 6 followed no.1 four or five years later. Construction therefore extended to four separate phases, not three: 21-28, then 1, then 2-6; and finally 7-14 & 15-20.**

Note that these events – the sale of no.21, building of no.1, and the following new deal for Archer and Gray – all took place in 1815, after Marshall Place had recovered from the disastrous flood of 1814.

**3 April 1815**    "The Council having considered a Petition of **Charles Archer** and William Gray for the Heirs of Bailie McEwan craving further time for building the lots of ground in Marshall Place and that the double feus *(feu duties)* stipulated by the Act of Council should in the meantime be dispensed with – and having taken into consideration that by the bargain then made with the feuars of Marshall Place by allowing an alteration of the original plan a considerable sacrifice was made by the Town *(see 6 January 1806)*, **as more money would have been got for the feus if they had originally been exposed upon the present plan** – and that the only consideration at that time required from the feuars by the Town for permitting the alteration of the plan was the condition of building on the whole ground within the period of years specified in that Act of Council, or of paying double feus in all time thereafter for such part as should not then be built upon, do therefore consider themselves well warranted to insist upon payment of the double feu, seeing the feuars have failed in implementing their part of the Agreement; yet in consideration of certain circumstances the Council are still willing to allow the feuars five years after Whitsunday next for completing the buildings in Marshall Place under condition that they shall, after expiry of that period, without further delay or excuse, pay double feu duty in all time thereafter for such part as may not then be built upon. And the Council declare that they will grant no further indulgence in that respect."

This casts some light on the legal and financial repercussions from the metamorphosis of Robert Reid's plans. For if "more money would have been got for the feus if they had originally been exposed upon the present plan" – i.e. more money was *not* obtained, because the only consideration at that time required from the feuars for permitting the alteration of the plan was the condition of building on the whole ground within the period of years specified in that Act of Council – then it becomes clear that the total revenue anticipated from the new scheme of 28 houses remained at the same level as from the original: 7 x £4 = £28.

Evidently, the original feuars, having imagined at the outset that they had pulled off a spectacular coup by securing for themselves these Lots for the building of large mansions – whether for their own patrician occupation or with a view to a speculative profit – but realizing within the next three years that the scheme was wildly over-ambitious, had obtained what seemed massive compensation by substituting the equivalent of four small house-plots for each large one (subject to the extraction of Nelson Street) with no increase in feu-duty, only to discover that this was no real consolation, for they still faced another nine years of commercial failure, compelling them to suffer the consolidation of their holdings eventually into the hands of only two proprietors, who in turn found themselves obliged to plead for this further reprieve.

So here is Charles Archer, ten years after acquiring Lot Third from Alexander Paul (see extract from title deeds below) and meanwhile also Lots Second and Fourth, pleading alongside the heirs to Bailie McEwan (who had acquired the other four Lots), for more time to get the houses built. Yet if it were still for only seven lots at four pounds per annum apiece, these two survivors must have been in dire straits financially to be so daunted by the prospect of its being doubled for another year or two – to a grand total equivalent to barely £11,000 par annum today!. But it is extremely frustrating that neither "the lots of ground" nor "building on the whole ground" nor "completing the buildings" is quantified.

Certainly, the Council was indeed generous, since the maximum period granted on **6 January 1806** was eight years from that Whitsunday (the May term or quarter-day) which had already expired. Furthermore, the feuars had undertaken that permission for the improved design would "ensure the same being immediately carried into execution"!

Once again, the 'certain circumstances' must surely refer to the wartime conditions: 3 April 1815 was just eleven weeks prior to the Battle of Waterloo – the outcome of the Napoleonic

War was still doubtful. Also, perhaps, there was some compassion for the heirs of Baillie McEwan, who must have died cursing the whole project, having seen no return on his purchase costs and feu duties for the accumulation of four Lots over the preceding twelve years. However, for the benefit of Archer and Gray, that latest deferment extended the development deadline only until May 1820.

It is hard to feel any sympathy for McEwan, however, having read this letter in the City Archives dated 6 April 1808 (PE15 Bundle 19), written by the Provost John Caw to McEwan's lawyer William Stewart:

*"Five or six people have complained to me to say that McEwan [McEwen] daughter of John McEwan had been for this fortnight laying on a stair-head in the South Street, starving and in distress, having been turned out by her father. You may recollect McEwan speaking to me about this daughter of his, in particular the day we inspected the Burn at Craigie….I wrote McEwan a note requesting him to keep his daughter off the street that she may not perish for want – as he is able to do – and I enclose you his reply refusing to do so – she must therefore come onto the public for surely she can't continue to be exposed to want while she is in distress and in the public street….profligate and debauched as she is. I know McEwan has had much distress and loss by her – yet still he is her father. Pray is it in the power of the magistrates to compel the father (as he is able) to provide for this poor wretch – depraved as she is?*

*Also I wish you would point out the proper steps to be taken – for I feel an inclination to enforce this on his refusal to comply with the request I made him. Tho' I wrote him, I did not do so as a magistrate. PS McEwan says his daughter is healthy, you'll observe, tho' that complained to me said that she was dreadfully ill."*

McEwan's reply was as hypocritical as it was inhuman: *"My Lord: I am sorrow [sic] that you have to be at so much trouble with any of my family but for me to dow mor nor I have done already I would consider it not to be my dutie as a parent. She is 17 years of age and a stout healthie woman and for me to ruin myself and family for her mor[sic] nor I have done it would not be consistent neither with the law of God nor man. I am sorrow at giving you so much trouble which I cannot help on that account. I am, Dear Sir, Yours etc, John McEwan."* What a monster!

A draft disposition in the City Archives refers to "Mrs Margaret McEwan otherwise Gray, eldest lawful daughter of the deceased Bailie John McEwan, Mason in Perth, & Spouse to William Gray, ironmonger in Perth", to Miss Jean McEwan, his "only other daughter" and to them as his "only children".

On 11 January 1820, McEwan's Heirs sold two house lots (not former "Lots" but the new house plots) to Daniel Carter for £180 and on 14 December 1824 they sold the house (no.1) on the corner to Mrs Margaret Dron or Stodart for £470. They needed to raise capital.

Again, a disposition dated 23 November 1819 recounts the sale by Charles Archer to William Gloag of two plots measuring 45ft. wide by 134ft. long for £200 "bounded by the tenement owned by William Gloag to the West and by ground owned by Charles Archer to the East". By now Archer, too, was desperate, while Gloag had become a power in the Town. How typical, by the way, that William Gloag married Janet Burn, a niece of James Paton, Thomas Hay Marshall's brother-in-law!

These plots eventually became nos.19 & 20, but were not developed by Gloag, as they lay fallow for another thirteen years.  Archer had not devised his plan for Nelson Street until late 1805, otherwise he could have confined himself to acquiring Lot Four, and not troubled with Two and Three, to which he had committed himself too early.

# Chapter IV

## TITLE DEEDS
### *– speculation and manipulation*

Let us pause here to examine the title deeds, starting with those for 21 Marshall Place, to understand the commitments entered into by the original feuars and how these obligations were varied by the wholesale changes in the development plans.

From the Disposition by Alexander Paul in favour of Charles Archer – dated 16th August 1805 and registered 4th May 1811:

"At Perth the Fourth day of May Eighteen Hundred and Eleven years In presence of Mr John Wright one of the present Bailies of the Burgh of Perth

Compeared John Miller Writer in Perth as and for the after designed Alexander Paul and gave in the Disposition underwritten desiring that the same might be Insert and Registered in the Burgh Court Books of Perth to the effect therein and aftermentioned which desire the said Bailie finding reasonable he ordained the same to be done accordingly and of which Disposition the tenor follows *Videlicit* Know all Men by these presents that

I Alexander Paul Merchant in Perth heritable Proprietor of the subjects after disponed for and in consideration of a certain sum of money advanced and paid to me by Charles Archer Merchant in Perth as the adequate and agreed on price of the said subjects after disponed, whereof I hereby acknowledge receipt and exoner and discharge the said Charles Archer and his heirs and executors thereof for now and ever have sold and disponed and do hereby sell alienate and dispone to and in favor of the said Charles Archer and his heirs and assignees whomsoever heritably and irredeemably all and whole that lot or piece of ground lying at the North end of the South Inch of Perth belonging heritably to the Community of the Burgh of Perth and within the Territory Royalty and Jurisdiction of the same, being marked lot third upon a Plan of the said South Inch and Spey Yards and grounds adjoining made out by David Buist Land surveyor in Perth *[1787 town plan]* and referred to in the articles of Roup after-mentioned with the whole Trees growing upon the said Lot, and Bounded the said Lot hereby disponed by Lot second sold to William Stewart Writer in Perth *[brother-officer with Marshall and Archer in the Volunteers]* on the West, by a street or passage of twentyfive feet in breadth to be made along the said Lots as laid down on the foresaid plan on the North, by Lot Fourth of the said ground belonging to James Ramsay Merchant sometime Provost of Perth on the East *[another brother-officer],* and by a Street of Fourty feet in breadth to be made along the said subjects as delineated on the said Plan on the South parts,  Together with free ish and entry to the said Lot of ground disponed by the said two Streets to be made on the South and North thereof, and with the burden and servitude upon the said South Inch that there shall be no building erected thereon in front of the Lot of ground hereby disponed within Four Hundred yards of the South front wall and railing to run along the southside of the said Lot as aftermentioned in all time coming together with all right title Interest claim of right property and possession which I or my authors or successors had have or any ways may have claim or pretend to the said Lot of ground hereby disponed in time coming  Declaring always as it is hereby specially provided and declared that the said Charles Archer and his foresaids shall be bound and obliged to erect a Building upon the said Lot of ground of dimensions and agreeable at least in the outward front roofs & gavel and in situation to the plans of the front and elevation and ground plan and section thereof, made by Mr **Robert Reid** Architect in Edinburgh of the building to be erected on the said Lot subscribed and referred to in the beforementioned articles of Roup.

The Fronts to be of ashler work and not to be more than two feet longer nor any shorter than the dimensions on the plans, that they shall raise the ground in front of the said House conform to the section thereof on the Plan marked Number first, Declaring also that the said Charles Archer and his foresaids shall be obliged to inclose the said Lot of ground and divide it from the adjoining Lots by walls and raills as underwritten those dimensions to be made and built mutually by them and the Proprietors of the Two Contiguous Lots.  That the wall and railling in front of the Lot disponed shall be made of the dimensions and as laid down on the said Plan Number first, similar to that at Athole Place and the division betwixt it and the Contiguous Lots, from the front railling as far North as the front walls of the House, shall consist of a similar wall and railling of the like dimensions, and a like wall and raill shall run East and West along the Lot disponed in a line with the front wall of the foresaid house

Declaring Further that the said Charles Archer and his foresaids shall not erect any other buildings on the said ground to the south of the line of the back walls of the foresaid house higher than the wall of the said division to run East and west in a line with the front wall, and that the Division walls betwixt the Lot disponed and those contiguous to the north of said division line running East and west, shall not be less than nine feet besides the foundations Which Lot of ground with the pertinents hereby disponed was exposed to public Roup by the Magistrates of Perth upon the Twenty fifth day of June Eighteen Hundred and Two years under certain Articles of Roup subscribed by them of that date at which roup I purchased the same and acquired right thereto by Feu Charter upon which I was duly Infeft.  In which Lot of ground with the pertinents I bind and Oblige myself and my foresaids under the conditions provisions and declarations before and aftermentioned duly and validly to Infeft and sease the said Charles Archer and his foresaids upon their own Expences To be holden of our Sovereign Lord the Kings Majesty & his royal Successors immediate lawful superiors thereof In free Burgage for payment of the Burgh Mails service of Burgh and others used and wont and that by resignation in manner under-written and also To be holden of the Magistrates and Town Council of the said Burgh and their successors in Office for themselves and in name and behoof of the whole Community of the said Burgh in feu farm fee and heritage for payment by my said Disponee and his foresaids to the Town Chamberlain of Perth and his successors in office for the use and behoof of the Community of the said Burgh out of and for the said Lot third, of Four Pounds Sterling in name of Feu duty yearly and that at the term of Martin-mass in each year beginning the first years payment thereof at the term of Martinmass Eighteen Hundred and Five for the year immediately preceding and so forth yearly in all time thereafter and Doubling the said Feu duty the first year of the entry of each heir and of each singular successor to the said Lot as use is in feu farm and that for all other burden exaction secular service or demand whatever excepting the Cess and other public burdens aftermentioned, and for expeding the said Infeftment by resignation I do hereby make and Constitute xxxxx xxxxx and each of them conjunctly and severaly my Procurators giving granting and committing to them and each of them full power warrant and commission for me and in my name to compear upon the ground of the foresaid subjects before the Provost or any of the Bailies of Perth for the time being and with due reverence by staff and baton as use is to resign as I do hereby resign surrender upgive overgive and deliver all and whole the foresaid Lot of ground lying at the Northend of the South Inch of Perth being lot third of the dimensions foresaid as delineated upon the foresaid Plan and as marked out upon the ground with the whole Trees growing thereon Bounded and described and with Ish and entry thereto and haill priviledges and pertinents thereof as above mentioned Together with all right and title thereto as said is But always with and under the Burdens Conditions Declarations & provisions above specified and here held repeated *brevatis causa*

In the hands of the said Provost and Bailies or their successors in office as in the hands of our Sovereign the Kings Majesty or his Royal Successors immediate lawful Superiors thereof beforementioned as to the Burgage holding and in the hands of the said Provost or any one of the said Bailies for himself and in name of the other Members of the Town Council of the said Burgh for behoof of the Community thereof superiors of the same as to the feuholding In favor and for new Infeftment of the same to be made & granted to the said Charles Archer and his foresaids heritably and irredeemably in due form Providing always as it is hereby specially provided and declared and to be insert in the Infeftment to follow hereon that if the said Charles Archer and his foresaids shall not make due and punctual payment of the said feuduty yearly but shall alow Two years to run into a third unpaid then and in that case they shall incur a forfeiture of the feuright of the said Lot of ground and of such buildings as may be erected thereon, and the said Town Council shall have power and liberty in that case to take possession thereof *brevi manu* without any action or declarator to be raised or execute for that effect and use the same as the property of the Community in all time thereafter or dispone thereof at their pleasure.

Acts Instruments and documents in the premises to take and generally every other thing necessary thereanent to do that I could do myself or that any other procurator might lawfully do or cause to be done in the like case promising to hold firm and stable all and whatsoever things my said procurators shall lawfully do or cause to be done in the premises and I bind and oblige me and my heirs & successors to warrant acquit and defend the said subjects hereby disponed this present right thereto and the resignation & Infeftment to follow hereupon to be good valid and sufficient free safe and sure to the said Charles Archer and his foresaids at all hands and against all deadly as law will and Moreover I make and constitute the said Charles Archer and his foresaids my lawfull Cessioners and assignees not only in and to the said Feu Charter granted in my favor by the said Magistrates of Perth and Instrument of Sasine following thereon of the foresaid subjects disponed with all clauses of warrandice and all other clauses and obligements contained in the said writes and all that has followed or may follow on the same, But also in and to the rents mail and duties of the said subjects from and after the term of Martin-mass Eighteen Hundred and Four which is hereby declared to be the time of entry thereto with power to him and them to ask crave uplift and receive the said rents Maills & duties and if need be to pursue therefor set raise output and input Tenants use warnings and prosecute removings and generally every other thing anent the premises to do that I could have done before granting hereof which assignation I bind and oblige me and my foresaids to warrant as to the foresaid writes and evidents at all hands and against all deadly and as to the rents mails and duties from my own proper facts and deeds only and also to free and relieve my said disponee and his foresaids of the Cess and all other public burdens affecting the same due at and preceeding the said term of Martinmass Eighteen Hundred and Four they being liable for and bound to pay the same and relieve me and my foresaids thereof in all time thereafter.

And I have herewith delivered up to the said Charles Archer the foresaid Charter granted in my favor by the Magistrates and my Infeftment following thereon. And I consent to the registration hereof in the Books of Council and Session Burgh Court Books of Perth or others competent therein to remain for preservation and that all execution necessary may pass and be directed hereupon in form as effeirs. And thereto I constitute xxxxx xxxxx my procurators. In witness whereof these presents written upon this and the three preceeding pages of Stamped paper by Thomas Scott Apprentice to Robert Peddie Writer in Perth are subscribed by me.

At Perth the Sixteenth day of August Eighteen Hundred and Five years before these witnesses the said Thomas Scott and William Roy Pearson also apprentice to the said Robert Peddie (signed). Alex Paul. Thomas Scott Witness. William Roy Pearson Witness. Extracted upon this and the Eleven preceeding pages by Robert Peddie."

Evidently, Alexander Paul bought the site from the Burgh Magistrates at auction on 25 June 1802 and only 2½ years later sold it on to Charles Archer privately ("in consideration of a certain sum of money") subject to the obligation to build a house in accordance with Robert Reid's plans and to an annual feu-duty of £4, the first payment due at Martinmas (the November term or quarter-day) 1805 for the year preceding. Accordingly the date of entry was the November term 1804 and the Disposition was executed on 16 August (the Lammas term) 1805. But of course these provisions related to the original scheme for one mansion house on each Lot.

Curiously, the document was drawn and witnessed by an apprentice to Robert Peddie, Charles Archer's Solicitor, the other witness being another of his apprentices, and signed throughout solely by Peddie himself, Alexander Paul's interest being represented only by the early reference to John Miller, Writer.

Curiously, too, Robert Peddie, a former Procurator Fiscal, on 13 September 1802 had been appointed one of Perth's three Principal [i.e. joint] Town Clerks, so that effectively he was representing the Council – i.e. the body that was both promoter and feudal superior – into the bargain! (Later, on the death of one of his colleagues he became Joint Principal with the other, upon whose death be became Sole Principal Town Clerk on 1 March 1813, entitling him to "the whole fees, dues, casualties, benefits and emoluments of the said whole office", which he held for the rest of his life – a powerful influence on the eventual progress of the development.)

These peculiar circumstances, coupled with the concealment of the terms of Paul's reconveyance to Archer, suggest that Paul had either bought the land speculatively with a view to taking a profit when the time was right or, on the contrary, had intended to build but had grown impatient at the lack of progress, or – most likely – simply could not raise the building finance. It certainly looks like a gamble gone wrong. For among Robert Peddie's private business papers in the City Archives (ref: PE52 Bundle 49) is a detailed statement dated 1808 of 'Creditors of Alexander Paul to Robert Peddie' from which he appeared to have been declared bankrupt, less than three years after the transaction with Archer.

That Minute of 3 April 1815 reveals that Charles Archer had also failed. His land speculation may have paid off in connection with the Methven Street extension (King Street) scheme, but apparently not here. Having owned the plot for almost ten years, including the period of eight years' grace that – despite securing approval for the improved plans – had already expired, and having now won yet another five years' extension, he could hang on no longer. For on 11 November 1814 he had already executed a Disposition for sale of 21 Marshall Place to William Gloag of Dunning at a price of £970 with settlement and entry on Whitsunday (May term) 1815.

But why should Charles Archer and Bailie McEwan's Heirs be "craving further time for building the lots of ground in Marshall Place", by Petition to the Council Meeting on 3 April 1815 – five months **after** Archer had contracted to sell no.21 and just a month before settlement? Doubtless because of loyalty to McEwan, his sole surviving co-feuar, and because, despite having actually completed building five (see below) adjoining houses some seven years earlier and having just succeeded in selling at least this one, he still needed several more years (and relief from double feu duty) in respect of the undeveloped land remaining from Lot Fourth.

*Now, from the Disposition registered on 4 March 1815 (every page of which is signed by the ubiquitous Peddie again acting for Archer, but George Condie representing William Gloag), referring to:*

"that tenement of land in Marshall Place as presently possessed by Mrs Stewart of Clunie with forty feet or thereby of ground in front and sixty feet or thereby behind or on the North of the said tenement with the buildings erected by me on the said ground, Bounded the said subjects hereby disponed by a road leading from East to West in front of Marshall Place on the South, by the tenement of land and other subjects sometime ago sold and disponed by me to the now deceased David Walker *[another former brother-officer in the Volunteers]* sometime cashier to the Perth Union Bank on the West, By a lane twenty feet wide running from East to West on the North, And by the ground still belonging to me on the East parts, Together with an equal right with me and my heirs and successors and the heirs and successors of the said David Walker to the mutual gavels *[gables]* and mutual walls on the East and West sides of the subjects hereby disponed and also with a right along with me and my foresaids to the Pit-well dug by me on the East side of the subjects hereby disponed, he and his foresaids being bound to pay a proportionate part of the expence of upholding the said Pit-well … the same being marked Lott third upon a plan of the said South Inch and Spey Yards and grounds adjoining made out by David Buist Land Surveyor in Perth and bounded the said Lott by Lott second sold to the now deceased William Stewart Writer in Perth on the West *[yet another member of this 'officers' club'!]*, by a street or passage of twenty-five feet in breadth on the North, by Lott fourth of the said ground purchased by James Ramsay Merchant sometime Provost of Perth on the East, And by a street of forty-five feet in breadth on the South parts …"   *[Note that the width of the back lane, originally planned as 25ft, had been reduced to 20ft.]*

*Final proof that Archer built the five houses nos.21 to 25 was provided by a title deed lent by friends who own no.25, which is described as occupying a piece of land* "twenty-two feet and a half in breadth from East to West and one hundred and fifty-four feet in length from South to North, together with the new tenement of land, being the Westmost of these five new tenements erected by Charles Archer, Merchant in Perth, who disponed the said subjects to David MacVicar sometime Merchant in Perth, upon part of the grounds now called Marshall Place, described in an Instrument of Sasine in favour of John  MacVicar…only son of the said David MacVicar deceased, dated and recorded in the Register of Sasines &c for the Burgh of Perth, the sixth February, eighteen hundred and ten;  bounded the said tenement and ground by the tenement and ground belonging to Bailie John McEwan, Mason in Perth, or his successors, in the West;  by a street of forty feet in breadth made along the front of Marshall Place on the South;  Partly by the tenement and grounds sometime belonging to the said Charles Archer, and partly by a lane of twenty feet in breadth which was to be common to the houses built or to be built by the said Charles Archer…"

*Also, other friends lent me a copy disposition for the sale of what became no.24, dated 12 May 1812, by* "Charles Archer to Mrs Bisset [Jean Keay relict of the deceased Patrick Bisset Coppersmith in Perth] & Daughters Helen, Marjory, Isobell and Elizabeth with consent of James Ramsay Merchant in Perth….by virtue of an Heritable Bond granted to him by the said Charles Archer …. That House lately erected by the said Charles Archer on that part of the South Inch of the City of Perth now called Marshall Place….bounded …on the West by another House…disponed by him the said Charles Archer to the late David McVicar Merchant in Perth and occupied at present by his widow….*" (subject to an annual feu duty of £2 – i.e. one half of the feu duty for the original Lot Second)*.  Miss Bisset and Mrs McVicar are both still listed in Leslie's 1837 Directory as owners of nos. 24 and 25 respectively.

*Among these title deeds for no.24 are those dated mid-1980s, after the property was divided, relating to ownership of the upper flats by Brian Souter and his sister, the future Anne Gloag, when they were starting what became the great Stagecoach business.   To digress further, her late husband was of the same family as William Gloag who (with his son) owned no.21 for half a century, as well as the famous distiller Matthew Gloag.*

Now, however, we know that Bailie McEwan's Lot First comprised only the first three houses (nos. 26-28) at the West end, to the corner of Scott Street, but we don't know how much Lot Third extended Eastwards from no.20.

Nor can we guess why Archer wanted to build and own five houses, in addition to that beautiful mansion on Victoria Street.  Besides, he cannot have made much profit, if any, from the sale of what became no.21, nine years after purchase of the site from Alexander Paul and seven years after completion of building.  The adjoining cases cannot have been any more lucrative.  Anyhow, as will be seen later, doubts arise as to whether even Archer's sale to Gloag was truly at arm's length.

My friends Reseda and Ian Muir, Perth architects and owners of No.23, lent me their own Disposition dated 9 September 1815, for the sale of that property by Charles Archer to John Miller, Writer.  Within a mere six months, Archer had sold both 21 and 23.  How curious that John Miller, Writer, who acted for Archer in his purchase from Alexander Paul, later purchased next-door-but-one for himself!

The division between Lots Second and Third is unclear, but Lot Second, originally bought (the very last Lot) by William Stewart Writer, is described by Archer as having been sold by him to the now deceased David Walker; therefore it must have been bought by Archer from Stewart and thereafter resold to Walker.  The feu charter in the Archives (PE76 Bundle 1) dated 15 July 1802 – following the public roup on 25 June 1802 – and registered on 13 January 1807, was indeed granted by the Town Council to Archer, but it reveals that the original purchaser had been William Stewart, who had duly paid the £200 at Martinmas 1803 but meanwhile quickly resold to Archer who subsequently sold to Walker. This was engineered because Stewart was McEwan's solicitor – so it reaffirms Archer and McEwan's joint venture in developing that whole first block.

***Furthermore, as we shall see shortly, Archer was in business with McEwan's son-in-law. Clearly, Archer was dealing in these plots wholesale; but why – in the absence of any demand and with no 'exit strategy'?  Archer seems to have been gripped by the same Marshall Place mania that had seized and destroyed Baillie McEwan.  Of course, Ramsay, Archer, Stewart and his successor Walker were not only proprietors in Marshall Place but were also, in 1805, fellow officers in the militia.  But by 1815 Archer was the sole survivor – not that he survived much longer.***

It did him no good that, whereas Bailie McEwan had boldly acquired the other four plots as quickly as possible, and retained them, the initial purchasers of Lots Four, Three & Two each resold quickly to Archer, almost as if they had been acting as fronts for his benefit.

*But the real estate interests – or, rather, their legacies – of both Archer and McEwan in Marshall Place extended still further. For a title deed as late as 1856, whereby parcels of land were sold by the Dundee & Perth & Aberdeen Railway Company and Aberdeen Railway Junction Company to the Eastern Bank of Scotland (presumably as security for loans), refers to:*

"All and Whole that Stance of Ground behind Marshall Place with the erections built thereon…on a Plan subscribed the Eleventh day of September Eighteen hundred and twenty three years *[John Wood?]* by the now deceased Patrick Gilbert Stewart Esquire, sometime Agent for the Bank of Scotland at Perth and Trustee on the Sequestrated Estate of Charles Archer sometime merchant in Perth to whom the said subjects sometime belonged in heritable Property, Bounded by Nelson Street on the West: by ground sometime belonging to the heirs of Bailie McEwan on the East; by a street forty feet wide on the North *[South William Street]*; and by a Lane running Eastward from Nelson Street behind the Eastmost Division of Marshall Place on the South…" (*i.e. 'Marshall Mews'*). This block provided one small section of the site for construction of the railway.

Why was the McEwan-Archer combine possessed of this compulsion to gamble against such ever-increasing building liabilities? (Long before the date of this deed, the remainder of Marshall Place had been completed by their successors, but the railways' acquisition of any other affected ownerships would have been the subjects of other deeds.)

The same railway title refers to: "*the ground purchased from Charles Archer's Sequestrated Estate by the late William Gray…*" Gray had no real option other than to consolidate his late father-in-law's holdings with Archer's, but maybe his heirs or trustees ultimately recouped some of his losses from the sale of such parcels to the railway company. Accordingly, to summarize the proprietary history:

1   Several individuals originally acquire the various feus;

2   Archer acquires three of them at second-hand, while McEwan picks up a couple more until he owns the other four;

3   McEwan dies and bequeaths all to his son-in-law William Gray;

4   William Gray in turn acquires some of Archer's holdings from Archer's Trustees in Bankruptcy;

5   Finally, the remaining vacant sites are sold on to builders in 1831.

## *Planned as a short-cut to riches – it became a road to ruin!*

*Archer's other interests had been even more widely spread. The Register of Sasines on 7 July 1811 details the Perth Foundry Company's purchase of:*

"parts of the lands of Blackfriars of Perth, on the North and South sides of Atholl Street and West side of Methven Street, with the houses and buildings thereon; on Disposition and

Conveyance by Charles Archer, Merchant, Perth, David Walker residing in Marshall Place of Perth, William Gray, Ironmonger there, and the Trustees of Davis Hood, Merchant there, partners of said Company."

Another contract dated 1816 between Robert Peddie as Town Clerk – as well as Clerk and Treasurer to the Goal Commissioners – and William Gray, Ironmonger, Charles Archer and John Archer, of The Perth Foundry Company, and James McEwan, Rope-maker, provided for them to undertake major refitting works on the Prison, designed by Robert Reid. Furthermore, William Gray had also became, with Charles Archer, a major proprietor (and casualty!) of Marshall Place. Is it not extraordinary that Archer and Gray, as well as David Walker, were all, not only co-proprietors in Marshall Place, but also partners in the Foundry business? The militia mafia surrounding Marshall Place was succeeded by a Foundry Company mafia. But all to no avail!

*Nevertheless, it is pleasing to reflect that the purchaser of the land, and eventual builder of No.21 was such a prominent figure and that his period of ownership (however ill-fated) extended neatly from the year of Trafalgar to the year of Waterloo. It is also gratifying that the first family to settle in the house was equally distinguished and that they lived here for half a century, until 1865.*

Villa in Marshall Place, Perth showing architectural details. Note the 'Lunette', one of Reid's favourite details.

# Chapter V

## THE PROJECT
### – and rogues' retribution

For William Gloag was a prominent banker, and in accordance with the Barons of Exchequer regulations, under the reformed local government regime from 1833, he was publicly elected the first Principal Collector of Assessed Taxes (and also, expressly and simultaneously, Sub-Collector!). In 1835 the Town published a volume which he edited: "Rentall of the County of Perth by Act of the Estates of Parliament of Scotland on 4 August 1649 – Contrasted with the Valuation of the Same County on 1 January 1835".

A survey plan by Henry Buist of 1791 shows the Feu of William Gloag in Granco, with the **"Outfields of West Findony"**, but that was his uncle. Then an entry in the Register of Sasines for 2 March 1815 records that John Gloag, Merchant, Perth, and his son William, acquired property "with teinds" (tithes) at "Thainsland or Glendunning which was called the Common of Dunning now Greenhill". Another entry for 16 April 1816 shows that "William Gloag of Common of Dunning and Janet Burn his spouse" acquired ground and building *"on the North side of Charter House Lane, being part of the Hospital Gardens of Perth; in security of £500, on bond and disposition by Charles Archer, wood merchant, Perth."*

Meanwhile, as early as 19 June 1808, Palliser of Dunkeld was writing to the Duke to advise that John Gloag, one of the 'linen stampers', wished to resign in favour of his son, William Gloag, if His Grace did not object, adding that Sir Patrick Murray was in favour. In the City Archives (B59/31/146) we find William Gloag by 29 September 1817 writing to the Commissioners of Supply, in his capacity of Depute Collector of Cess, petitioning for a monetary allowance "for the trouble and risk" which he had to run in collecting – as he took pride in pointing out – £1,166.19.4 each year.

James Paton wrote formally to the Duke on 18 January 1818 to advise that William Gloag, Deputy Collector of Land Tax and Assessed Taxes, had been appointed by the Barons of Exchequer as Interim Collector of Assessed Taxes and was a likely candidate for promotion to full Collector, if the Duke did not object to his holding both Collector's offices – to which there was no legal impediment in Scotland although it did not accord with 'English' practice. Of course, as we know, William Gloag had married Paton's niece!

So Gloag was well qualified to drive a hard bargain with Archer. But as we shall see, there was far more to it than that. For Archer's continuing predicament, even after disposing of Lot Third, is amplified by the next relevant Council Minute:

**3 May 1819** "There was laid before the Council a Petition of William Gray Ironmonger and Charles Archer Merchant stating that the petitioners or their authors about the year 1805 feued from your Honors a number of stances of grounds at the North end of the South Inch of Perth, each stance or lot to pay four pounds of feu duty, That by minutes of your Honors of date 6 January 1806 it was made a condition of the feus to the Petitioners that they should build houses agreeably to a specified plan upon the grounds so feued betwixt *[blank]* and *[blank]* and with certification that if they failed so to do they should be liable in double feu duty, That the Petitioners accordingly finished a considerable number of houses prior to the said *[blank]* but their being no demand for them the Petitioners found that it would be a great loss were they obliged to compleat the remainder in the time specified. They therefore applied to your Honors praying that the time allowed for compleating the plan should be prorogated in the hopes that the demand for houses of this description would encrease and on those grounds your Honors were pleased to extend the period till the term of Whitsunday next. That the Petitioners' sole object in purchasing the different stances was, that they might build upon them for Sale and it was evidently for their interest that this should be done as soon as possible – the stances themselves yielding no revenue and the Petitioners being subjected to a great annual loss – That the Petitioners therefore used every exertion to get the houses, which they had already built, sold. But this has not as yet been altogether accomplished and even now some of them are standing empty. However that they might shew their anxiety to get the plan completed they last season proceeded to build and have now nearly finished Six additional houses and there is hitherto no prospect of any of them being sold or even Let. In these circumstances and as it is their intention to get on with the building as speedily as possible the Petitioners hope your Honors will not insist on exacting the double feu duty. May it therefore please your Honors to take the Petitioners' case into consideration and as the annual loss on the ground as it now lies is a strong stimulus on them to complete the plan as soon as possible, your Petitioners hope you will be pleased to withdraw the Certification contained in the Minutes first above mentioned and to allow such time for completing the buildings as the demand for houses of this description may render necessary. (signed) William Gray / Charles Archer"

"The Council upon taking this matter into consideration Agree to prolong the time for building upon the remaining stances in Marshall Place until the term of Whitsunday Eighteen Hundred and *[blank – but the next extract indicates that it must have been a three-year extension to Whit 1823]* But under this Certification in the original bargains and former Minutes of Council that they should be liable in double feu duty for such part of the grounds as may not then be built upon, agreeably to the specified plan."

The six new houses referred to in that last Minute are the corner house which was built on its own in 1815, and the next five built in **1819**, comprising the second and third phases shown as one block on John Wood's plan of 1823, representing modern street nos.1-6.  But how many of those first eight houses (nos.21 to 28) were still standing empty twelve years later?

Had the William Gloag family several neighbours by then, or did they still dwell in solitary splendour?  It is likewise impossible to quantify *"a number of stances"*, *"a considerable number of houses"*, *"completing the buildings"*, etc.  But why should Gray, considering the disastrous inheritance from his father-in-law, want anything to do with that third phase – and who on earth was persuaded to finance it?

How amazing, also,  that Archer was still able, as late as in 1819, to promote a petition to the Council as a responsible house-builder, considering the following lengthy extracts from a monumental memorandum among the 'Daily Accounts of Robert Peddie 1813-1815' in the City Archives (PE52 Bundle 51):

"Mr Gloag holds a promissory note of the Perth Foundry Company dated 1815 for £1,180, in consequence of further sundry articles have been attached on the Foundry business to the amount of £1,544.14.0.  Of this Bill there is no entry whatever in the Foundry Company's books, the Factor [?] cannot therefore state either the exact amount or the date of this Bill.  But he can state with confidence that the only sum at Mr Gloag's credit in the Foundry Company's books is £500....in consequence of an entry in the Journal of date 31 December 1819, of which the following is a copy*:*  John Archer's New Account due to William Gloag, for the sum transferred, £500.'  *(This entry, tho' standing in the Company's books of the above date, was only written, amongst a great variety of other entries, a few days before the Foundry stopped payment.)*

Mr Gloag has for many years been on terms of great intimacy with Mr Charles Archer*,* the Father of John Archer, and also one of the Partners in the Perth Foundry Company**,** and entered into **a great speculation with him in building houses** *[Marshall Place – but no mention of the salient fact that Archer had, just weeks earlier, sold him his family home (No.21), ostensibly at a price of £970, for that was probably a device for settling debts.].*  In the course of this transaction with the Father, it is not doubted that Mr Gloag has advanced several large sums of money to the said Charles Archer, which he was well enabled to do, being a man in affluent circumstances.  But this money so advanced by Mr Gloag has no connection with the Public Money, nor is the Crown in reality in any way concerned, Mr Gloag having repeatedly, since the date of the Bill on which he founds, cleared with the Exchequer.  Had Archer's debt to Mr Gloag been contracted since Mr Gloag's last Settlement with the Exchequer, and arisen from public money in his hands as Collector of Taxes, there might have been some apparent ground for this plea, tho' Mr Gloag himself in every way able to fulfil his engagements.  His securities to the Crown are underwritten.

**But it is apprehended that Mr Gloag made an unwarrantable use of his situation as Collector of Taxes in thus attempting, after Charles Archer has been made bankrupt**, to recover what was originally a *bona fide* and private debt, under service of (a Writ of) Extent *[an instrument to secure priority for government agencies over private creditors]* to the manifest injury of Creditors at large. It is not improbable that after the advances to Charles Archer had become considerable, the said Charles Archer had given Mr Gloag the security of the Foundry Company – and it is but fair to state that for the last two years Charles Archer and Son have credit in the Foundry Books for the sum of £59 in each year, being interest paid on this new Account of John Archer's, and which would make the principal to have been £1,080 *(at 5% p.a.)*.

But then 'John Archer's New Account' never had credit in the Foundry Books for more than £700, of which £500 was, as before stated, transferred to Mr Gloag as on 31 December 1819, and the remaining £200…to Mr William Dickson. So far then as concerns Mr Gloag, there is no word in the books of any other sum than this £500, and it is apprehended that the remainder of the debt he claims must belong exclusively to C Archer or C Archer & Son.

With regard to Collector Malcolm's debt, there is no appearance of it in the books. He is the Father-in-Law of John Archer; and if from time to time he may have been induced, from that connection, to advance money to his son-in-law, whether in part of what he was to have given as his Daughter's portion or otherwise, it is conceived it would be a gross abuse of his situation as Collector of Excise to attempt to recover those sums as a debt to the Crown – indeed it is well known that the Collector at first expressed his abhorrence of such an attempt, and that he has only been induced to alter his determination on finding that Mr Gloag has taken the steps that he has done."

**That final comment from the magisterial Robert Peddie sounded a decidedly ambiguous note – almost a verdict of 'Not Proven' on William Gloag's conduct in seeking to recover the money due from the Archers. What a parlous state for young Archer: pursued both by his father's banker and business partner who happens to be the Town's Collector of Taxes and by his own father-in-law who happens to be Collector of Excise – he collects Collectors!**

The rival creditors sound like two competitors in a walking race who have both broken into a run, each fearing that otherwise the other would do so first. Small wonder, considering the desperate state of the Foundry Company's finances as revealed by Robert Peddie's notes, which calculate total indebtedness as £26,927.03s.5½d and a free fund of only £813.04s.6d, permitting a dividend (after allowing for fees, etc.) of only 6¼d *[2.7p]* in the £. Indeed, the foundry had foundered!

So William Gloag may have effectively bought 21 Marshall Place with his own money! But what was Charles Archer doing, still representing himself as a respectable and substantial businessman, shortly after he had been bankrupted? Or had he meanwhile – within that short space – somehow extricated himself, if only temporarily? Had one of his cronies bailed him out – but why should any of them do so, since they were all in the same sinking boat?

The mystery of Archer's precarious survival is intensified still more by the discovery that, as a timber merchant, he was commissioned by the Duke in 1818 to supervise the construction of a brig made of larchwood at James Brown's shipyard in Perth. George Condie drew up the contract and William Gloag was banker, of course. Archer duly advised in October 1819 that 'The Larch' had been successfully launched and was lying afloat at Friarton *[on the Tay]*, awaiting His Grace's further orders, so by December 1820 he triumphantly reported that she had sailed from London to St Petersburg five months ago, where she took on a cargo of hemp and flax for Oporto, and a cargo of wine for London, arriving in excellent condition.

He added that she had outsailed everything else she had met except for one French brig; only once had to use the pumps during the passage from Oporto to London and all the masts except the topmast had stood the strain. So here is Charles Archer, gaily ship-building for the Duke yet bankrupt – along with Thomas Anderson (Marshall's father-in-law) and Alexander Paul, among others.

What a contrast to the fortunes of the carefully calculating William Gloag, whose civic eminence is obvious from a hand-written Minute [PE54] of a Meeting held on 21 February 1820 of the special 'Committee on Provost Marshall's Monument' shows those attending as Provost Morison, William Gloag, Major Sharp, N Lindsay and Wm John Sandeman. It reads:

*"Smirke's plan to be adopted – Unanimously. Application to be made to the Town Council for permission to erect the Monument in the North Inch which the Committee think be much the best situation in the neighbourhood."*

An earlier entry in the Register of Sasines for 20 June 1811 details a purchase of ground on the West side of Methven Street by the Foundry Company, the original feu charter having been granted by the trustee on the Sequestrated Estate of Thomas Anderson, Merchant, Perth, to James Wyllie, Alexander Paul and James Caw, Merchants, Perth, on 2 November 1799, the disposition and assignation "by the trustee on the Sequestrated Estate of Alexander Paul & Co, Merchant, Leith, and Alexander & John Paul, the individual partners thereof, with consent of the said Alexander Paul, formerly Merchant, Perth, of his third share of the said Foundry Company."

**So all first three owners of 'Lot Third' – Paul, Archer and Gloag – as well as William Gray (as successor to Bailie McEwan) and the late David Walker, had all five shared a common interest in the Perth Foundry Company as well as in the development of Marshall Place! This dual association was almost incestuous and certainly ruinous for most of them.**

Found in Perth's Archives (PE16 Bundle 57) is a Solicitor's Account between Charles Archer and David Morrison dated 1819: "To Cash advanced on the Heritable Security of a House *[that's the full description!]* 7 July 1812", plus Interest calculated to 7 July 1819, amounting to £244.03.06, with the contra entry dated 14 September 1820 – "By the above Heritable Property Sold this day by Public Roup and purchased by David Morrison £200, leaving Archer £44.03.06 out of pocket." Evidently he had owned it for seven years but never paid for it.

1819-20 were indeed the years that destroyed him. Was the house one of those that he had built on Marshall Place – there was no D Morrison listed in that 1837 Directory, but could it have changed hands again meanwhile? The first Post Office Directory, for 1845-46, shows 16 changes out of the 28 listed in that first Leslie's Directory only 8 years earlier! At all events, Archer clearly was conducting a 'fire sale' – a price at auction of precisely £200 suggesting that there were no other bids.

Another paper in the City Archives dated 13 April 1820 (B59/40/265), entitled 'Valuation of Buildings & Grounds belonging to Charles Archer, Wood Merchant, Perth', shows that he had owned a vast estate (but no doubt heavily indebted) on the South side of the city, comprising almost all the land and buildings between Canal Street and Marshall Place, excluding the McEwan's holdings which were mainly concentrated towards the Princes Street end. For example:

"That Lot of Garden Ground presently occupied by John Bunton, Gardener, with the house thereon bounded upon the North by the foresaid 56 feet wide *[future Victoria]* Street, upon the South by the foresaid 40 feet wide *[future William]* Street, upon the East by Nelson Street and upon the West by Grounds belonging to the Town of Perth – value £240." *This was the whole block behind the Western terrace in Marshall Place, between William and Victoria Streets. The final five items of this Inventory are of special interest.*

"That Lot of vacant ground behind Marshall Place bounded upon the West by Nelson Street, upon the East by grounds belonging to the heirs of Bailie McEwan, upon the North by the foresaid forty feet wide street and upon the South by the lane running from Nelson Street eastward behind the eastmost division of Marshall Place. Value £40. Yearly feu-duty 10/-" *(50p: i.e. 1¼% p.a.) This parcel was later acquired by the Railway Company.*

"That vacant front stance in Marshall Place forming the corner house upon the East side of Nelson Streeet with the background behind the same, bounded by Nelson Street on the West, by the property belonging to William McEwan's Heirs on the East, by the aforesaid lane behind Marshall Place on the North and by the street leading along Marshall Place on the South parts". Value £90. Yearly feu-duty 20/-." *(£1: i.e. 1.1% p.a.)*

This is clearly the Lot on the East corner of Marshall Place and Nelson Street. So Archer had owned the whole block from Marshall Place back to William Street and Eastwards from Nelson Street to the McEwan ownerships.

 "That corner stance fronting Marshall Place and ground behind the same on the East, on the West by Lot 15/21 *[a different notation]*, on the North by the lane running westwards from Nelson Street behind Marshall Place and by the street running along Marshall Place on the South. Value £90 – feu duty 20/-"

This is clearly the Lot on the West corner of Marshall Place and Nelson Street, therefore another part of Lot Four, given that Archer owned only nos. Two, Three & Four. (That is corroborated by another paper in the Archives (B59/25/2/207) which lists feu duties payable (but no longer directly recoverable) by Charles Archer to the City "at Martinmas yearly" in 1821-22, including "Lots 2, 3 & 4 Marshall Place: £12." This confirms that Lot Four did indeed originally contain the whole frontage embracing what became the Marshall Place end of Nelson Street.

So Archer definitely conveyed to the Council the section required for the formation of Nelson Street, whether for a substantial or a nominal sum, but certainly ensuring that the new dividing street was laid out at public expense on land that he owned, to form an avenue forming an imposing approach to his grand villa on Victoria Street.

"3 vacant stances on Marshall Place lying betwixt the Houses already built and the corner stance above described with back ground thereto belonging, bounded on the East by Lot 14/21 [?], on the North by aforesaid lane behind Marshall Place, on the West by the property belonging to Mr Gloag and on the South by the aforesaid street in front of Marshall Place. Value £150 – feu duty 60/-" *(£3 – i.e. 2% p.a.)  This is within Lot Four extending towards what is now No.20 Marshall Place, but whether that was included or formed part of Lot Three has yet to be determined.*

"That lot of vacant ground behind the feus of Marshall Place and bounded by the aforesaid lane behind Marshall Place upon the South, by the foresaid 40ft wide street upon the North, by Nelson Street upon the East and by the property of the heirs of Bailie McEwan upon the West. Value £180." *This section, later acquired by the Railway Company, lay behind the Eastern terrace, extending from Nelson Street as far as the McEwan property at the Princes Street end.*

To recapitulate: why did Marshall's disciples, having burnt their fingers over the grandiose original scheme for seven large mansions, embark with equally indecent haste – and still with no thought of market research or development appraisals – on what was a far more speculative development?  And did not the honest citizens wonder that such imprudence – not to say incompetence – was displayed by those in charge of their Town?  For, given the scale of the new scheme, the capital receipts and feu-duty income were inadequate, the project had proved a folly twice over and an economic disaster for all those enticed by it, yet nobody dared complain publicly.

How could these houses possibly sell, given not only the destitution of the country but also its continuing civil unrest?  James Paton wrote to the Duke from Marshall Cottage on 24 December 1819, to report that Patrick Stewart of the Bank of Scotland, accompanied by the ubiquitous William Gloag had conducted a house-to-house canvas to find recruits for the Armed Association or Volunteer Corps but had enrolled only 52, of whom most were elderly or unfit, so he was deferring the exercise pending heightened public alarm.  Besides, the estimated number of radicals in Perth was only 150 and most of them were grateful for any relief given.

He wrote again on 9 April 1820, commenting on recent radical disturbances and on the Stirlingshire skirmish with the Hussars and Stirling Yeomanry, which had "intimidated their friends in Glasgow, who are reported to have returned to work and become peaceable…All was remarkably quiet at Perth." *This sounds suspiciously like putting the best face on the situation for the benefit of His Grace.*  The weavers had again petitioned the magistrates to find them work. The young and able will have to find work for themselves as best they can and the aged and infirm will have to be put on the "ordinary list of the poor in Perth, supported by an Assessment, as the asking of more voluntary funds meanwhile is considered inappropriate and unavailing."

It is significant that no figures were ever mentioned in these recurring petitions to the Council from Marshall Place feuars.  Construction costs were not quantified, nor were selling prices quoted.  The inferences are that these local personages were anxious to conceal the parlous state of their finances and that, in any event, price was not a factor, for the houses simply would not sell.  Considering the recent insolvency of the Perth Foundry Company, the next Minute is equally surprising.

**3 March 1823**  "There was produced and read to the Council a Petition by William Gray Ironmonger in Perth *(Charles Archer having meanwhile gone bust)* for the Heirs of the late Bailie John McEwan there, regarding the feu duty of the lots of ground in Marshall Place, which as a compulsitor to building were declared to bear double feu in case they were not built upon within a certain period from the time of the original Charters, but which period for building had been extended by the Council formerly in consideration of the little demand for Houses in that quarter, and the hardship of obliging Feuars to expend money in the building of houses which were not likely to be tenanted, but the time to which the indulgence for building had been extended by the Council being now elapsed, Mr Gray made the present application for a further prolongation of the period, stating that, although Bailie McEwan's Heirs had two years ago erected two expensive tenements in Marshall Place, yet no tenants could be found for them and they still remain empty, the Council, upon consideration of this and being satisfied of the facts stated in the Petition, and of the hardship of the case, Agree to prolong the time for building for Seven Years after Whitsunday next Eighteen Hundred and Twenty Three."

*This latest extension granted by the Council was the fourth in our sorry saga:  from 1806 to 1814, 1815 to '20, '20 to '23, and now to May 1830.   A quarter century of deferments so far – and it's not over yet!*

As we saw earlier, the "two expensive tenements" had been built between 1816 and 1820.  But once again, given the lack of demand and the financial straits of the promoters, how could the capital have been raised for the construction of these second and third phases?  That Eastern end may have been considered the more desirable and valuable than the remoter, cheaper Scott Street end.  Certainly, these modern street nos. 1-6 must have comprised the whole of the original Lots Six and Seven.

The Town Chamberlain's Accounts for the year 1830-31 show payments credited to "John McEwan's Heirs" of £16 for "Four Lots of Marshall Place" (i.e. £4 apiece) but divided equally between John M.Gray (William Gray's representative) and David Greig.  So two of these four Lots must have comprised the "two expensive tenements".

Yet another entry credits David Greig with the feu duty for "the corner stance on Marshall Place  £1.12.00" *(£1.60: i.e. 2/5ths of £4)* and for "the small stance 16/-" *(80p: i.e.1/5th of £4)* which must relate to the corner of Princes Street within Lot Seven.

These Accounts provide further clues.  For they show payments of feu duties in respect of houses within the first phase, built on parts of the original Lots but before they were given the street numbers from 21 to 28.  Thus, a payment by William Gloag, who owned no.21, is noted as for "1/5th part of Lot Two and 2/5ths of Lot Three £2.08.00". (i.e. 3/5ths of £4.) Therefore, now we know that Lots One and Two comprised street nos.22-28. Again, Miss Bisset is credited with payments of 16/- for "1/5th of Lot Two"; and we know from Leslie's 'Directory' that she owned no.24. (16 shillings being 1/5th of £4.) Likewise, Mrs Vicar, whose house became no.25, is also credited with "1/5th of Lot Two". Entries for 1826-29 indicate that Miss Bisset and G. Stewart were acting as Charles Archer's Trustees in paying off his "arrears of feus and seat rents".

As always, the lack of specification throughout official records is utterly exasperating. However, the Town Council's Rentroll, including Feu Duties, for the year from 30 Sept. `46 to 1 Oct.`47 (the first complete annual record available) leads closer to a resolution of the mystery. For it lists all the Marshall Place feuars as follows. Remember there were 12 pence to a shilling and 20 shillings to a pound.

| 1 | Mrs MacVicar | £0 .16s.0d |
| 2 | Miss Bisset | 0 .16 .0 |
| 3 | Charles Sim | 0 .16 .0 |
| 4 | Cameron & Gelletley | 0 . 6 .4 |
| 5 | William Gloag | 2 . 8 .0 |
| 6 | James Rollo | 0 .16 .0 |
| 7 | William Cleland | 0 . 9 .8 |
| 8 | William Gray's Heirs | 1 .12 .0 |
| 9 | William Cleland | 0 .16 .0 |
| 10 | Mrs Cleland | 0 .10 .0 |
| 11 | Andrew Graham | 0 .14 .6 |
| 12 | John Stewart | 0 . 7 .6 |
| 13 | Daniel Carter | 1 .12 .0 |
| 14 | John McEwan's Heirs | 8 . 0 .0 |
| 15 | David Greig | 8 . 0 .0 |

*Twenty years earlier, David Greig (or his father?) had been Town Treasurer. Thirty years earlier one D. McVicar was Town Chamberlain (the old title for the same office), but there may be no connection.*

**The number of fifteen and the odd sums of feu-duty appear, at first, unrelated to the situation. They seem to complicate everything still further, until it is realized that the total amount is precisely £28.00.00 – i.e. 7 x £4, which was the feu-duty for the original seven Lots!**

So nos.14 and 15 each comprised the equivalent of two Lots, nos.9-13 one Lot, nos.1-4 plus just over half of no.5 comprised another and nos.6-8 plus just under half of no.5 the other. Note also that, in addition to the £8 for McEwan's two Lots, the Grays were liable for another 2/5ths of one Lot.

Meanwhile, the decline in fortunes is illustrated by the Town Chamberlain's Accounts dated 29 September (the annual accounting date and Council Elections day) 1827, which note the following receipts: "John McEwan's Heirs' feu duty £15.17.6" (*for their four Lots – though why not the full £16 is unclear*) and "Charles Archer's Creditors seat rents & feu duties £23.16.2" (*no doubt including for their four Lots*). By the way, the civic purse remained heavily dependent on rents from seats in the Town's churches: in that year alone producing the colossal sum of £8,338.18.7!

**1 March 1830** "There was produced and read to the Council a Petition by Messrs Robert Morton, Tanner, and David Greig, Watchmaker, narrating that they had purchased the remaining vacant stances in Marshall Place *[when, precisely, from whom and for how much?]* and had already commenced building thereon, agreeably to the plan, but in respect of the impossibility of finishing the said houses before Whitsunday next, craving that the Town might extend the time within which the said stances should be built on for another year without any increase of the feu-duty. The Council....resolve and agree to extend the time for building the said houses till the term of Whitsunday Eighteen Hundred and Thirty-One, with certification that if the same are not then built on the whole feu-duty stipulated by the Charters of the said subjects shall be exacted."

So this was the fifth extension. William Gray, on behalf of McEwan's Heirs, had now fallen by the wayside. (Nevertheless, the family ironmongery business continued, for in the City Art Gallery is a small picture of their shop at no.7 George Street, trading under the appropriate name of John McEuan Gray.) Incidentally, the great David Octavius Hill, pioneering photographer and painter, was born in Perth in 1802, the son of a bookseller with a shop at 23 George Street. Hill was one of the founders of the Royal Scottish Academy in 1829, serving as its Secretary for the next forty years. In 1821, at the age of 19, he had published probably the first set of lithographs produced in Scotland, 'Sketches of Scenery in Perthshire'.

Morton and Greig must have had money – if only we knew what (how little?) they paid for all those remaining empty plots! Evidently, another year or two's grace was added, allowing for completion of the two terraces in **1832-33**. Indeed, a Minute dated **4 February 1833** shows that residents were already asserting themselves.

"There was produced and read to the Council a Representation by certain inhabitants in King's Place and Marshall Place complaining of the trees in the Inches being made use of for hanging and drying clothes and the Council having deliberated on this subject they remit to the Magistrates to prohibit by printed handbills the appropriation of the young trees in the Inches for that purpose and also to prohibit Sailors and others from hanging cobles or other parts of the rigging of their vessels on the trees adjoining the Shore."

## *A Parallel Chronology*

The economic difficulties throughout the Napoleonic Wars and their aftermath, which so bedeviled the development of Marshall Place, were precisely paralleled by Reid's Second New

Town in Edinburgh, where the 1ˢᵗ phase from Heriot Row to Dublin Street was finished in our commemorative year of 1808, but Great King Street was not finished until 1823 and the final phase covering India Street and Royal Circus not until much later again.

Small wonder that Robert Reid's scheme for an extension westwards of his terraces was still-born. The intention was to build between Scott Street and Hospital Lane – later renamed James Street – and beyond to King Street (these two blocks forming the future King James Place) and beyond again to Paradise Place, to form, confusingly, the future King's Place. His drawing of a "Ground Plan" (RHP 30112/ NRAS 268 36 4) held in West Register House, formerly his own St George's Church, is inscribed: "This plan occupies the ground of the front lots as marked *[followed by 13 lot numbers]* on the original feuing plan", but presumably the sale or roup was cancelled or failed, since the land was not built upon for another fifty years after completion of the two terraces – notably, of course, by the great church of St Leonard's-in-the-Fields, designed by J J Stevenson and built in 1882-85, extending from Scott to James Street.

That block was laid out on Reid's plan in typical fashion as a double unit on each corner of 39'0" frontage, embracing four singles of 21'9"; then the block to King Street comprising corners again of 39'0" embracing four of 22'6"; but a variation for the block to Paradise Place, comprising large corners of 47'0" and a centre of 36'6" flanked by two at 19'6" on each side.

A wonderful aerial projection of this scheme, as it would have appeared, is revealed in William Brown's painting of "Perth from Barnhill" *[page 26]*, dated 1831 – a couple of years before the hasty completion of Marshall Place – for by then there was no hope of its enlargement.

No. 14 Marshall Place, Perth. Used as the office of Muir Associates Architects (At the time of writing).

# Chapter VI

## ROBERT REID
## *– the great unknown architect*

Why should a 23 year-old architect, of whose early life and career so little is known, suddenly appear from Edinburgh in 1797 to start work with Marshall's father-in-law on plans for Perth's 'Northern New Town' and five years later be chosen by the City fathers to design (first) the scheme for seven large villas and (second) these two great terraces, along the new road facing across the South Inch?

These Perth commissions coincided with his equally surprising success (from a short list of four) in the competition conducted by the George Heriot Trustees in conjunction with Edinburgh Council to plan and lay out Edinburgh's Northern New Town across a large portion of the Heriot Estate. Reid was in the throes of that competition when he received the summons to Perth. Thomas Anderson may not have expected him to win it – his triumph there followed the Marshall Place commission by only a matter of months – but suddenly Reid found himself with two monumental jobs on his hands.

The large-scale master-planning of the 'Second New Town' necessitated a far longer 'lead-in time' than for the Perth projects where municipal control ensured a much earlier start on site. Nevertheless, his sudden fame in the capital must have influenced Thomas Anderson and his son-in-law, whose recommendation to Perth Council proved decisive.

The Edinburgh Northern New Town scheme, undertaken in collaboration with architect-builder William Sibbald (about whom little more is known) was a colossal project, to double James Craig's first New Town by extending it down the hill from Queen Street Gardens northwards to Fettes Row and Royal Crescent and eastwards to Bellevue Crescent, creating magnificent townscape as in Heriot Row, Great King Street, Drummond Place and London Street. Furthermore, in 1802-3, he designed the headquarters building for the Bank of Scotland.

Finally, in those halcyon years of 1802-03, he secured the most lucrative and illustrious commission of all, from the Trustees for Public Buildings in Edinburgh, that was to provide work for the next 35 years – the extension to the Law Courts and redesigning the frontage to

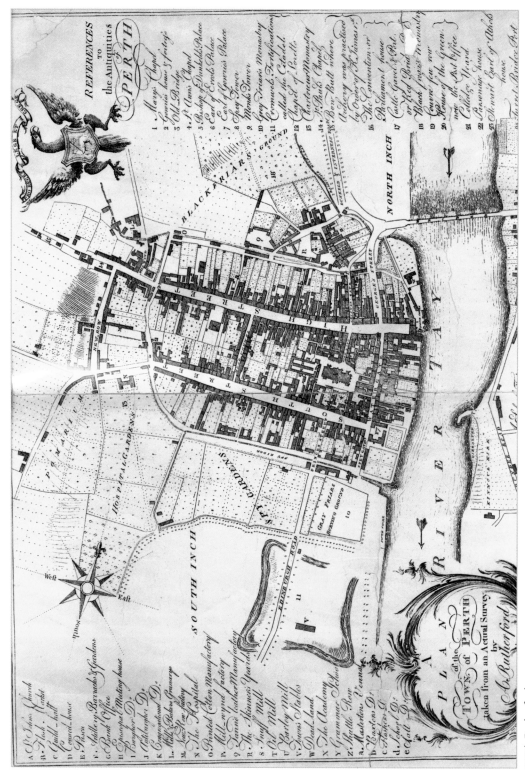

1 Mary's Chapel
2 Gowrie house & 3d Entry
3 Old Bridge
4 S.t Anns Chapel
5 Bishop of Dunkelds Palace
6 Earl of Errols Palace
7 Earl of Gowries Palace
8 Spey Tower
9 Monks Tower
10 Grey Friars Monastery
11 Cromwels Fortifications called the Citadel
12 Chapel of Loretta
13 Chartreux Monastery
14 Parish Chapel
15 Bone Butt where Archery was practised by Order of K. James
16 The Convention or Parliament house
17 Castle Gavel, y.e Port or Red Brod
18 Black Friars Nunnery, near the Post Office
19 Gowrie for ever House of the Green
20 House of the Green
21 Callender Ward
22 Sessation house
23 Stewart Earl of Atholls house

NORTH INCH

RIVER TAY

BLACKFRIARS GROUND

HOSPITAL GARDENS

SPY GARDENS

POMARIUM

SOUTH INCH

GRAY FRIARS BURYING GROUND

West
East

PLAN
of the
TOWN of PERTH
Taken from an Actual Survey
by
A. Rutherford

A S.t John's Church
B Flesh Market
C Guild hall
D Council house
E Prison
F Artillery Barracks & Gardens
G Bank Office
H Principal Meeting house
I Burgher D.o
J Antiburgher D.o
K Congregational D.o
L Milk & Bakers Granary
M New factory
N The Hospital
O Provost Colton Manufactory
P Mill, wright factory
Q Turnic leather Manufactory
R The Skinners Yard
S Snuff Mill
T Oyl Mill
U Barley Mill
V Omnis Stables
W Dead land
X The Academy
Y Grammar School
Z Skittle Room
a Masters Pennam
b Baxters D.o
c Flaxers D.o
d Short D.o
e Coll D.o

1774 Rutherford

Parliament Square, creating an open square around St Giles Cathedral and incorporating the superb Signet Library (although that was the work of William Stark and Playfair).

The main work was carried out in 1807-10 but continued until much later, interrupted by a great fire in 1824.

In 1808, the year of Provost Marshall's death, Reid somehow found time to design the New Court House in Inverary, while acquiring new work in Perth – including the Prison (1810-1812) and County Buildings (1812-14) – as well as in Edinburgh, where he was responsible for extensive improvements around the Palace of Holyroodhouse and went on to design the Lunatic Asylum (1809-10), the vast St George's Church in Charlotte Square (1811), now West Register House, and the classical Customs House in Leith (1810-1812). Worthy of special note is the unique, neo-classical Picture Gallery and Library – his finest interior – at Paxton House, Berwickshire (1813). He designed Wick Town Hall (1825), planned the sea wall North of St Andrews (1825) and worked on St Andrew's University College's East range during 1829-31. Restoration work on Arbroath Abbey and Elgin and Glasgow Cathedrals was undertaken in 1834-36. This was altogether a phenomenal output, especially considering that the bulk of it was carried out during the Napoleonic Wars and its aftermath of destitution.

Just as lucrative as Parliament Square, and as influential in advancing his reputation, was the commission to design the Northern extension to Robert Adam's Register House which further overloaded his office from 1822-1834. Reid's attention to his terms of employment was notorious. He wrote on 1 October 1822 (the heading was simply "George Street") to Thomas Thomson, Register House Clerk: "I am not quite sure if I ought to say anything *[but was obviously determined to say a great deal!]* on the subject of my own remuneration in the business. I think there can be no doubt but the Trustees will consider the work in question as a case of extraordinary business and not included in my duties or small salary as ordinary surveyor to the Building, and that for the performance of this extraordinary business, that is in the making out the details, working drawings and superintending and directing the execution of the new work, examination and adjustment of the tradesmen's accounts of it, I shall be entitled to the usual fees of my profession. I will of course have the same duty as at present to perform as surveyor in the matter regarding the old portion of the Building, and the erection of the new Building must I humbly conceive [?] be considered as altogether additional. This is all that I could have wished to have submitted to the Trustees and as I cannot be present tomorrow *[the reason given was that he was "still so very lame"]* you will oblige me very much if you would merely mention the matter to them."

Public buildings in Scotland in the 18<sup>th</sup> century were under the control of the Scottish Court of Exchequer. The post of Master of Works had long been a sinecure and the old organization of the Royal Works in Scotland had fallen into abeyance. But in our golden year of 1808, Robert Reid, who was already working on the Law Courts in Parliament Square, obtained a commission authorizing him to adopt the title of "King's Architect and Surveyor in Scotland". The office was purely honorific, but Reid determined to make it a reality. So when England's Surveyor General of Works visited Edinburgh in 1821 (accompanying George IV),

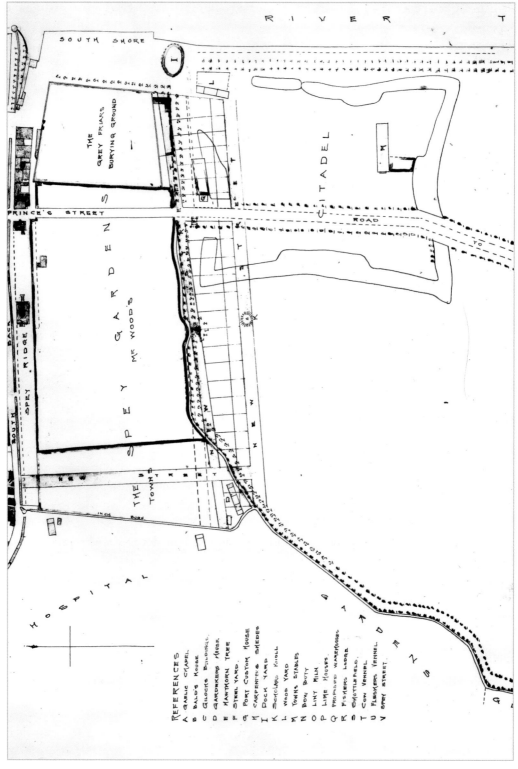

REFERENCES
A GAELIC CHAPEL
B BALD'S HOUSE
C GILOCK'S BUILDINGS
D GARDENERS HOUSE
E HAWTHORN TREE
F STEEL YARD
G PORT CUSTOM HOUSE
H CARPENTERS SHEDES
I DOCK YARD
K SCHOLARS KNOLL
L WOOD YARD
M TOWNS STABLES
N BOW BUTT
O LINT MILN
P LIME HOUSES
Q PROPOSED WAREHOUSES
R FISHERS LODGE
S SHUTTLEFIELD
T COW VENNEL
U FLESHERS VENNEL
V SPEY STREET

1787 Buist

Reid – having secured the Register House appointment – seized the opportunity to persuade him that a Scottish Office of Works (similar to England's) should be established, with responsibility for all public buildings – including those of the judiciary and the revenue as well as the Crown.

No action was taken, but when the titular Master of Works (James Brodie) died in 1824, Reid succeeded in getting that office merged with his own. As "Sole Master of our Works and General Inspector and Overseer and Architect and Surveyor of all our Palaces and Public Buildings of whatever kind in Scotland" he was accorded a salary of £200. Then in 1827 a Scottish Office of Works was duly established, with staff and an office in Parliament Square and his salary raised to £500, back-dated to 1824 – *why?* However, in 1840, as one of Melbourne's cost-cutting measures, that Office was abolished and Reid was retired – he was nearly 65 – but on full pay, which he continued to enjoy for another 16 years…..long enough to see the Scottish Office of Works regaining its independence in 1851.

He was a pioneering conservationist, declaring: "I conceive that in all cases of this kind, restoration or embellishment should not be the object…but that repairs should be executed with a view solely to their preservation."

*(Since Reid practised prior to 1840, his work falls outwith the scope of David Walker's monumental 'Dictionary of Scottish Architects', so recourse was had to Howard Colvin's equally Herculean 'Dictionary of British Architects 1600-1840', from which some of the above is quoted.)*

Yet, despite that unrivalled body of work and renown, Reid remains a mysterious figure and strangely uncelebrated. He was born on 8 November 1974 in Edinburgh, the son of Alexander Reid, mason and builder in the Tron Kirk parish, and his wife Mae Cochrane.

Reid senior had been Deacon of the Masons from 1787–91 and had feued lands in the New Town. Indeed, he was a substantial developer, responsible for the two blocks at the West End of Princes Street and sections of Charlotte Square, York Place and elsewhere in the New Town. By 1799 both father and son were styling themselves Architects. They lived for a while at No.18 South Castle Street, and by 1811, after his father's death, Robert settled in 44 Charlotte Square (within the block comprising 33-46 which he designed), where he died on 20 March 1856, having spent most of his retirement at his country house, Lowwood, at Gattonside between Galashiels and Melrose. On 26 September 1832 he had attended Sir Walter Scott's funeral at nearby Dryburgh Abbey. He was survived by his wife Sarah (née Wisdom).

His estate included numerous individual houses producing good rentals, but with no apparent investment strategy – 25 York Place, 18 Maitland Street, 18-20 Young Street and 72-74 George Street among them, presumably acquired at random as a safe haven for his surplus funds. His personal estate amounted to above £1,000 and under £1,500, therefore attracting a stamp duty of £30, and included the "Proportion of retired allowance due to the deceased as Architect and Master of Works in the late department of HM Office of Works for Scotland for the period from 1st January 1856 – £101.2s.0d – Deduct Income Tax £5.17s.10d = £95.4s.2d."

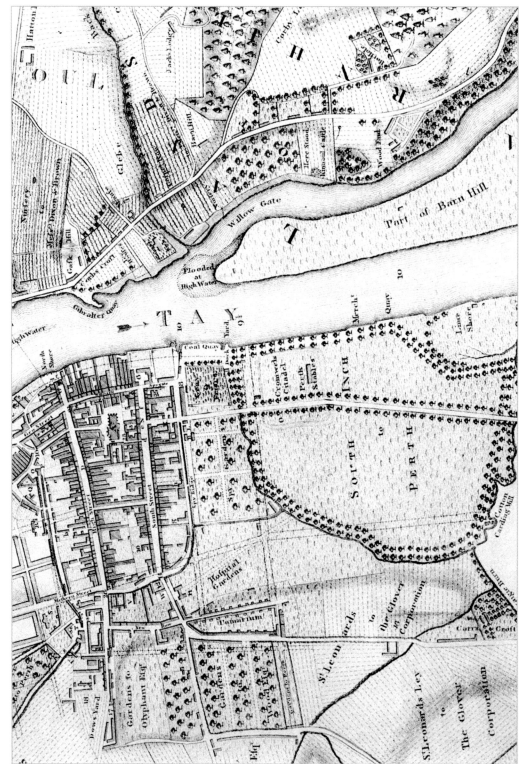

1792 Macfarlane

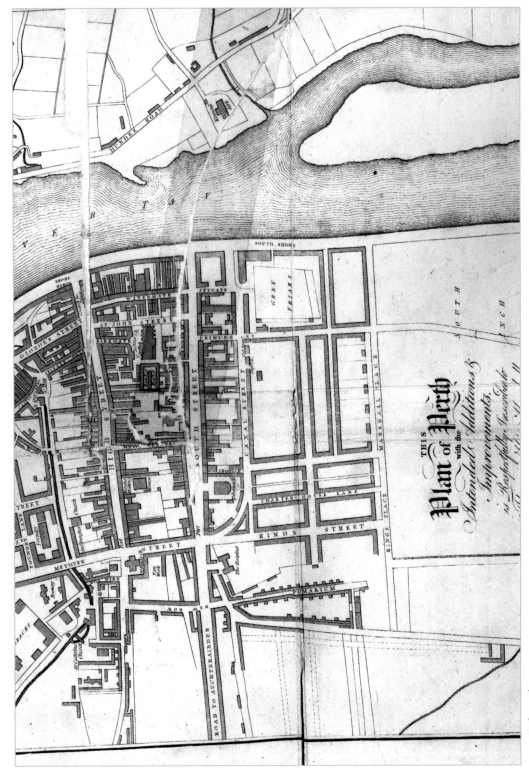

1805  Kirkwood

Evidently, even when aged over eighty, he still enjoyed a retirement pension of more than £450 p.a. – a very comfortable income.

His buildings have been widely criticized by contemporaries and by modern authorities alike. '*The New Edinburgh Review*' in 1823 reflected a common opinion: "Have we not a right to grieve at…the new Church in Charlotte Square…We have no less reason to lament the tastes which produced the Bank of Scotland." The Bank was described by Henry Cockburn (after whom the Cockburn Association – Edinburgh's Civic Trust – was named) as "a prominent deformity"; by Sir John Macdonald as "really an eyesore". Colin McWilliam in his '*Edinburgh*' ('*The Buildings of* Scotland', Penguin, 1984), wrote of St George's Church: "Robert Reid adopting Adam's 1791 scheme of portico, dome and flanking pavilions, but making it bolder in mass and simpler in detail – the latter no doubt in the cause of economy. His rash verbal estimate was £18,000, but even with further savings the cost had risen to £23,675 when the church was opened in 1814. 'It is certainly a pity that the Adam design was not used', said the '*Scots Magazine*'." To quote the old aphorism, comparing St George's with the beautiful but inconspicuous St Andrew's Church at the E end of George Street, 'St George's is the wrong church in the right location whereas St Andrew's is the right church in the wrong location'!

A J Youngson ('*The Making of Classical Edinburgh*', 1966) deplored the Parliament Square design: "It is a competent piece of work, but monotonous and rather undistinguished. To those who knew the old building and revered its 'Scottish architecture', Reid's design was a nonentity…and for them the contrast was all the more painful. In his '*Memorials*', Cockburn expresses some of the indignation felt at the time, describing 'The Parliament Square (as foppery now call it, but which used, and ought, to be called the Parliament *Close*)', he wrote:

"The old building exhibited some respectable turrets, some ornamented windows and doors, and a handsome balustrade. But the charm that ought to have saved it, was its colour and its age which, however, were the very things that caused its destruction. About 170 years had breathed over its grave grey hue. The whole aspect was venerable and appropriate; becoming the air and character of a sanctuary of Justice.

But a mason pronounced it to be all '*Dead Wall*'. The officials to whom, at a period when there was no public taste in Edinburgh, this was addressed, believed him; and the two fronts were removed in order to make way for the bright freestone and contemptible decorations that now disgrace us."

Youngson also criticized Reid's northern extension to Register House: "it must be said that the total effect is somewhat ponderous." The same epithet is used by Colin McWilliam, describing The Law Courts as "Ponderous Adamesque wallpaper by Robert Reid, 1803-38, hems in the small civic space to the N *[he meant S]* of St Giles". McWilliam likewise derided Reid's Customs House in Leith as "Brutalist". Not surprisingly, Youngson concluded that "a sigh of relief must have gone up… when [Reid] failed to secure the job of completing the University."

Naturally, fierce competition raged among architects during this period of rapid

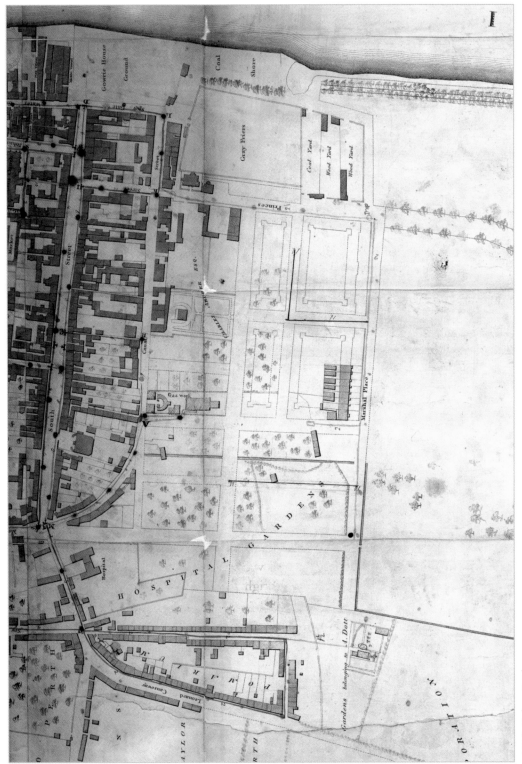

1809: Robert Reid

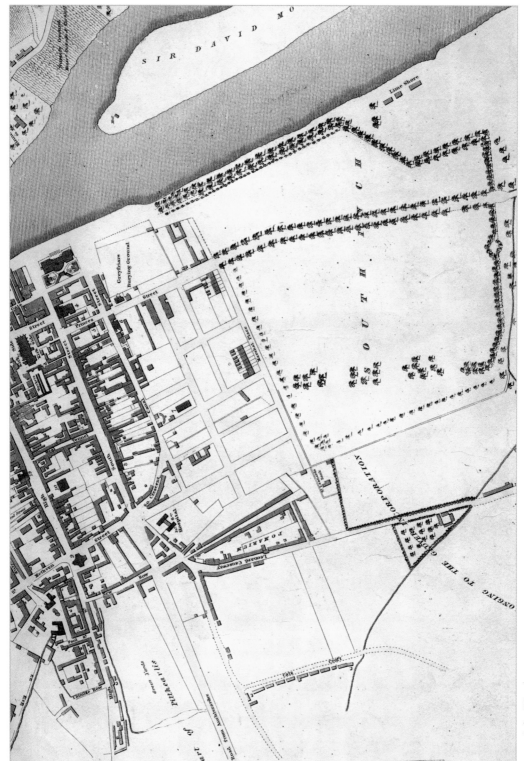

SIR DAVID MO

SOUTH INCH

Lime Shore

Greyfriars Burying Ground

Street

Princes Street

Street

Vennel

South Street

High Street

Methven

Row

Canal Crescent

PONMIUR

Leonard Causeway

CORPORATION

Cats Croft

ONGING TO THE

Green Yards

Pithea v lif

Thistle Row

Road from Auchterarder

1823 John Wood

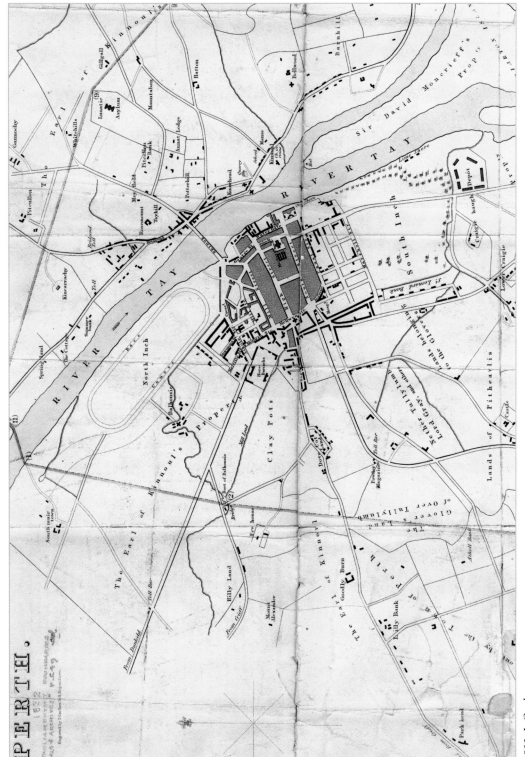

PERTH.

1832 J. Gardner

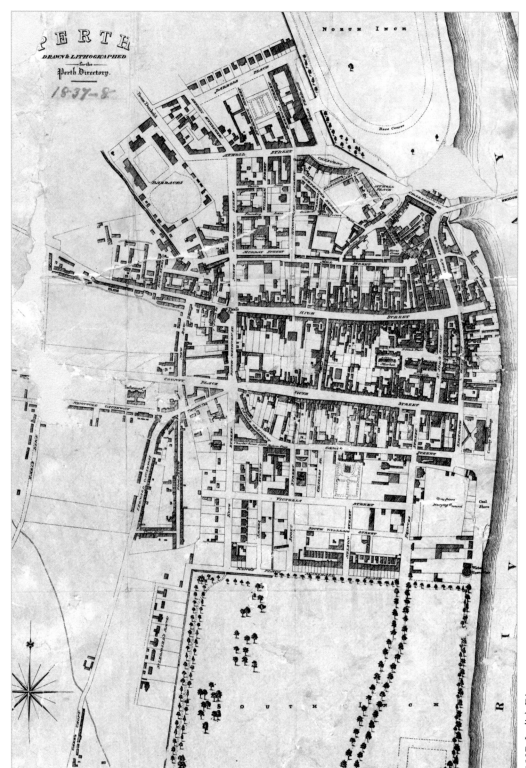

1837 Leslie's Directory

development in Edinburgh.  By all accounts, William Burn and William Playfair were at one another's throats, while, according to Rebecca M Bailey's *'Scottish Architects' Papers – A Source Book '*(Rutland, 1996):  "few appeared to like Robert Reid; James Gillespie Graham (1777-1855:  an almost exact contemporary!) was considered a vulgarian and Burn considered Thomas Hamilton a man of low taste."  She also derides Reid's office of King's Architect & Master of Works as a "somewhat artificial incumbency", while Charles McKean describes him (Oxford Dictionary of National Biography, 2004, vol.46) as: "This prickly, somewhat self-important, old-fashioned, but dedicated architect".

The inscription on his monument in Edinburgh's Dean Cemetery reads:

 "For XXXIII years Crown Architect for Scotland – who by his eminent professional abilities no less than by his private virtues secured the warm esteem and lasting friendship of a large circle of the most distinguished of his contemporaries".  As McKean laconically adds: "It would be good to know who those were."  The inscription across the plinth of the tombstone is equally incongruous:  *THE MEMORY OF THE JUST IS BLESSED".*

There's the paradox: he was apparently difficult and many of his major works suffered obloquy; yet he was astonishingly diligent and prolific and always in great demand (especially in Perth) and, despite his modest origins, enjoyed constant royal patronage.  Despite his long life, despite his eminence from the reign of George III through those of George IV and William IV into the Victorian era, and despite his having done much of his best work in those early years, yet we still know so little about the man.

Yet this whole book could have been entitled "Robert Reid and the Rebirth of Perth" for his work on Marshall's Northern and Southern "New Towns".  He certainly deserves belated elevation to the pantheon of Great Scots.  How better to commemorate him than by celebration of the bi-centenary of these two terraces in Marshall Place, his first major commission and most outstanding achievement in the city which possesses the greatest concentration of his work outside Edinburgh?

**The most appropriate date is surely 2008, the bi-centenary of both the completion of the first phase (nos. 21-28) and of Thomas Hay Marshall's death.**

'The Marshall Monument' (Perth Museum and Art Gallery's Ionic portico) – *building designed by David Morison (1823) – memorial by James Ness (1890)*

# Chapter VII

## ENVOI
### – the final chapter of privilege

The Marshall Place conspiracy may seem a parochial affair of little consequence, but actually it was of national significance, as a demonstration of the dying powers of the Scottish *ancien régime.* The fourth, final phase of building those twin terraces was in progress during the passage of the monumental Reform Act of 1832, which released the clamour for parliamentary and local government reform that had been suppressed, ever since Pitt the Younger's far-sighted yet defeated proposals of 1785, by the establishment's fears of revolution. Different revolutions – the agricultural and industrial – were in full swing, Napoleon had been vanquished and Britain was supreme maritime power with an expanding colonial empire, but civil unrest was widespread, especially in the North and Midlands of England and in Scotland, fomented by radical elements and aggravated by fierce Tory opposition to any extension of the franchise. So the demand for greater democracy had to be met, otherwise a popular uprising – precisely what reactionary forces feared – would have become irresistible.

As Tom Devine wrote in *'Scotland's Empire'*: "Scotland seemed especially ripe for reform. After the Union there were forty-five parliamentary seats in the Scottish counties and fifteen elected from the burghs, each with 2,600 and 1,500 voters respectively. This tiny electorate was around 0.2 per cent of the Scottish population in the later eighteenth century. Even by the pre-democratic standards of the day, this extraordinary concentration was unusual. Both England and Ireland had much larger franchises; Dublin's alone stood at 2,000 to 3,000 and by itself exceeded the total county electorate in Scotland. Initial stirrings of reform came in the burghs during the 1780s, followed in the wake of events in France by the Scottish Friends of the People Associations which were first established in 1792."

Likewise, T. C. Smout in *'A History of the Scottish People'*: "The United Scotsmen, a small and shadowy secret society advocating annual Parliaments and universal suffrage, and maintaining contact with the United Irishmen, operated from 1797 until 1802. Their ringleader, George Mealmaker, who was arrested in 1797 and received the usual sentence of fourteen years' transportation, was a weaver of Dundee. Their complete failure to start anything of significance even in the year of the Militia Riots [1797] underlined again both the success of the government's repression and the uninflammable character of the Scottish populace as a whole."

Devine also comments: "the régime emerged unscathed from these challenges. Despite the enormous changes in Scottish society during these decades, no basic change in the country's structure of governance took place until the Reform Act of 1832."

It is almost incredible that this enclosed, oligarchal system persisted throughout Marshall's life and for another twenty-four years after his death. No wonder the Marshall Place conspirators could exploit their positions and hush up their machinations with such impunity!

Perth had a population of some 14,800 in 1801, rising to some 19,100 in 1821, and continuing to grow rapidly through the economic revival of the 1830s. Smout paints a glowing picture of the preceding period: "Perth was perhaps one of the most interesting of all provincial towns at the end of the eighteenth century, for it borrowed almost equally from the characteristics of Edinburgh and Glasgow: it was renowned on the one hand for its academy, its assemblies, its genteel society and its literate interests, and on the other for its linen industry, its cotton work at Stanley, its boot and shoe manufactories, its paper mills, its printing works and its exports of fresh salmon refrigerated on blocks of ice for the London market."

There are interesting parallels, incidentally, between the development of Marshall Place and of Stanley Mills. They suffered similar vicissitudes throughout this turbulent period. The Stanley Mills Company was founded in 1785 by the Duke of Atholl's grant of a feu over 70 acres within the peninsula formed by the River Tay, around which the water level fell by 21 feet, generating immense power. The seven original partners, who each invested £1,000, were Richard Arkwright, George Dempster MP, William Sandeman (the elder, owner of the Luncarty bleachfields, who died in 1790 to be succeeded by William junior, both being connected to the Andersons), Patrick Stewart, William and Andrew Keay, and young William Marshall, who died three years later. So the Bell Mill was built in 1786-87 and the East Mill in 1792-93, but they closed a few years later as the French Wars caused a slump. They were also ravaged by fire in 1799. (Dempster complained of losing £8,000!)

In 1801 they were bought, then repaired and reopened, by James Craig, a Glasgow muslin manufacturer, for £4,600, provided by David Dale, founder of New Lanark Mills and Robert Owen's father-in-law. But failure once again forced closure in 1813 with debts of over £40,000. It was not until 1823 that they reopened, following acquisition by Buchanan & Co. of Glasgow, who then built the Mid Mill and extended the East Mill, ushering in more than a century of fluctuating prosperity.

Perth was indeed the first Scottish burgh to erect an academy (see 'Seminaries'), thanks to a report presented to Perth Town Council as early as 1760 by the Rev. James Bonnar, in which he prophetically advocated that: "In times long past, all learning was made to consist in the grammatical knowledge of dead languages….but Providence has cast our lot in happier times, when things begin to be valued according to their use, and men of the greatest abilities have employed their skill in making the sciences contribute…to the improvement of the merchant, mechanic and farmer, in their respective arts…The people of England have…private academies established in almost every great town where not only the languages but those sciences which are of the greatest use in life are taught in a compendious and practical manner."

But this cultured and enterprising surface concealed not only radical ferment but also what it fed upon – destitution among sections of the fast-expanding urban population as well as a tyrannical State, whose absolute power was exercised by the aristocratic landowners in league with a reactionary judiciary and self-serving local government. Dramatic improvements in agricultural technology from the 1780s onwards had transformed large areas of the rural economy, but the benefits were only beginning to filter into the towns when the Napoleonic Wars imposed even more severe hardship and curtailment of liberties. It is astonishing, therefore, that Marshall and Reid achieved so much during those first few years of the nineteenth century, in face of the most hostile political and economic conditions.

But they did not know that, once their work was done and peace had returned and the whole country was prospering again, their private world of Perth – their exclusive fiefdom – would have gone for ever. They could never have imagined that Marshall Place, born after such a painful, protracted gestation, would survive as a magnificent memorial to the last generation of municipal privateers.

That era of embryonic, still vulnerable, democracy, and a rising mercantile middle class, had begun just a hundred years earlier, replacing mediaeval princely patronage as the source of culture and mercantile power after the Glorious Revolution in 1688-89 and Treaty of Union in 1707. But now, in 1832, was born the age of empire and national institutions. Culture and mercantile power for the next hundred years (until the Wars of the 20th century) depended largely on the new species of enlightened capitalist who also promoted great architecture, mainly in a spirit of philanthropy. Since 1945 that source has been exhausted by the State, leaving architecture – and culture generally – in the hands (or the tight fists) of bureaucrats. Maybe the buccaneers of two hundred years ago were not so bad, after all! Certainly, within that historical context, it is clear that Marshall Place perfectly illustrated that great divide of 1832. With the old city behind, it looked across the South Inch, facing an unknown modern world.

On a bizarre footnote, the Perth Museum holds a Petition to HM King George V, praying for an end to the torture by forcible feeding of suffragettes on hunger strike in prison. This Petition had been thrown at the King's person by one of these female agitators in Marshall Place.

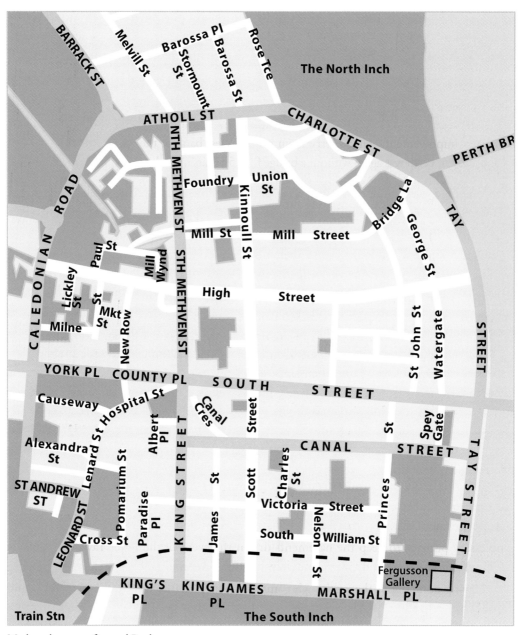

Modern day map of central Perth.

My late, dear friend and close contemporary Colin McWilliam described Marshall Place in *'Scottish Townscape'* (Collins, 1975) as "a representative masterpiece of the early 19th century art of town improvement.  First a ferry town on the West bank of the Tay and then for a time a bridge town, Perth was again without a bridge for 150 years until the opening of Smeaton's bridge in 1771.  This permitted the expansion of Perth, both to the North and the South, presenting the Provost and Magistrates – and Robert Reid – with these splendid opportunities for urban grandeur.  McWilliam further commented that Marshall Place **"faces South Inch in a manner which immediately recalls Reid's work in Edinburgh, skilfully scaled down;  a double terrace like Great King Street, but relying for its effect (as in London Street) on simple planes and characteristic semi-circular windows in the attic storeys of the end blocks."**

McWilliam's collaborator, Professor David Walker, kindly commented on the design of Marshall Place, that "the resemblance to Reid's Drummond Place/ Great King Street scheme was once closer than it is now.  As in London Street the original design did not have Ionic pilasters.  Reid's [Edinburgh] scheme was enriched by Thomas Bonnar and later Thomas Brown as architects to the city.  The resemblance would have been still more marked if the [Perth] scheme had been built consistently in the fine white Fife sandstone used in the original houses *[i.e. 21-28 & 1-6]*.  This was probably shipped from Cullaloe near Aberdour, which could be expensive.

The later houses, contrary to conditions of feu, used a local and unreliable red sandstone which has had to be painted or cement-rendered in places.  It may be vain to look for a waiver in the feu charters; it may have been done 'on the nod' rather than in writing.  Interesting that Marshall Place has front gardens when Reid's New Town terraces do not.  It may have been done to help keep the terraces level; if so the banking of the site would be quite expensive, but necessary perhaps to keep the basements dry in the event of the River Tay being high:  cf. Gillespie Graham's later Howard Place [close to the Water of Leith]."

Having pointed out that, although commissioned in 1801, Marshall Place was still under construction in the early 1820s *[actually, into the '30s]*, Nick Haynes described it in *'Perth and Kinross – an Architectural Guide'* (Rutland Press, 2000) as:

**"two monumental palace block terraces of houses, which in their heyday would have rivalled the great development schemes of Edinburgh's 2nd New Town, Glasgow's Blythswood and Aberdeen's King Street-Union Street.  Reid's distinctive attic lunettes mark the centres of the main blocks and pavilions."**

But he goes on to lament that, sadly, the unity of the scheme is now barely discernible, following removal of astragals, truncation of chimney stacks, addition of dormers and painting of individual elevations (not to mention removal of front gates and railings).

The above two references chime with this passage from A J Youngson's *'The Making of Classical Edinburgh'* (EUP, 1966):

**"In Aberdeen, Union Street, George Street and King Street were laid out and Union Bridge built in the early years of the nineteenth century. Perth, taking advantage of the new opportunities provided by Smeaton's Bridge, opened George Street in 1772, Charlotte Street, going west from the bridge and leading to much early nineteenth-century building and on to the Dunkeld Road, in 1783, while elegant Marshall Place, facing the South Inch, began to be built in 1801."** *[actually, not until 1806, as you know]*

Colin McWilliam was also Founding Editor with the great Nikolaus Pevsner of the 'Buildings of Scotland' series, in collaboration with Professor David Walker and John Gifford – the latter of whom produced the superb, long-awaited 'Perth & Kinross' volume, published by the munificent Yale University Press in 2007 (ISBN 978 0 300 10922 1), in which he reports:

"Nos.1-14 and 15-28…are a pair of thirty-one-bay palace-fronted blocks designed by Robert Reid in his heavy-handed Adamish manner in 1805 but not completed until 1831 *[1832]*. Each has slightly advanced and pyramid-roofed three-bay end pavilions of three storeys and a basement, joined by ten-bay, two-storey, attic and basement links to a five-bay, three storey and basement piend-roofed centrepiece. Sober adornment at the pavilions and centrepiece whose ground-floor windows are round-headed and overarched; round-headed overarches also at the doors but the tops of these arches are filled by fanlights. Console-corniced first-floor windows at the inner pavilions (Nos.14 & 15) and centrepiece. At the second floor, small windows and a central Diocletian window (a lunette at Nos.21-22).

Over each of the pavilions and centerpieces, a blocking course, rising to a parapet at the centre. Ball-and-spike finials survive on the roofs of Nos.15 & 28…."

***So we shall finish with 'finials'!***

*Appendix 'B'*

*Modern Times: Values stagnating and soaring*

William Gloag is listed in the local Post Office directory as the house-holder of No. 21 as late as 1855.  After his death, the house passed in May 1865 to his son, John Austin Gloag (Writer of Dundee) who promptly sold it the following month for £570, barely half what had been ostensibly paid fifty years earlier – which is further proof that the original price had been a sham.   (Incidentally, subsequent Gloag executorial records show continual interplay between Williams and Matthews.)

Another 20 years later, advertised for sale by auction on 19 March 1885 (the year that the great church of St Leonard's-in-the-Fields was built), it was sold at the upset price (reserve) of £800; and was advertised again for auction on 2 September 1903 at an upset price of just £1,000 – which it failed to realize.  It sold again in 1929 (the year of the 'Wall Street crash') for £800 – the same figure as for 44 years earlier – and for an abysmal £780 in 1946, when the property was dilapidated after the War.

Thus, over the 131 years from the end of the Napoleonic Wars to the end of the last one, the value barely kept pace in nominal terms, and fell in real terms to roughly one quarter.  For after two World Wars, a social revolution marked by the disappearance of domestic staff, continuing dependence on coal, and no property maintenance for over 40 years, there was no demand for near-derelict 4-storey houses in a country town.  So some were converted to office use and many to bed-and-breakfast establishments catering mainly for 'commercial travellers'.

No. 21, for example, sold for only £1,575 as recently as 1971, improving to £4,400 in 1972 after modernization, then rocketed to £20,000 in 1975 after conversion to a guest house, £34,000 in 1979, £40,000 in 1982, £47,000 in 1985, exploding tenfold over the next twenty years, through the housing market booms of the late '80's and '90's, reinstatement as a private residence and historical restoration.

How ironic that the original developers were ruined because there was no viable demand for these houses then – nor even 150 years later – and only now, after two centuries, they have come into their own!

# Glossary

ASHLAR — Building stone with carefully hewn and wrought facings

BAILIE — A Councillor serving as a Magistrate

DEACON — The President (or Convener) of one of the incorporated trades or crafts in a Scottish town or city

EXCAMBION — An exchange of land, often a 'give-and-take' to straighten boundaries (also to simplify negotiations)

FENCIBLES — Civilians, not volunteers but fit and liable for military service at home (*'defence'*)

FEU *('fee')* — A perpetual tenure of land granted to a 'vassal' subject to an annual 'feu duty' payable to the 'Superior' (ground landlord) and to any special conditions/restrictions in the 'Feu Charter'. If granted for building purposes, a capital sum (a premium or *'grassum'*) was also usually demanded.

FRIARS — Four Orders each had monasteries in Perth. The Burial Ground at Tay Street-Canal Street is where the Greyfriars (Franciscan) monastery stood. Blackfriars Street and Wynd, by the North Inch, commemorate the Blackfriars (Dominican) monastery site.. The Whitefriars (Carmelite) was to the West (at Tullylumb), and The Charterhouse (Carthusian) was at the junction of Hospital Street and King Street, replaced by the King James VI Hospital (built 1748-52).

LADE — A channel for leading water to a mill-wheel

SEISINS — *('seize')* The title deeds to feudal property

SUPERIORITY — The absolute ownership of land (held of the Crown) from which subordinate feus were created — hence the proprietorship of an estate

TURNPIKE — (turnpike road) A public highway subject to payment of tolls